2010 JOINT STRATEGIC PLAN ON INTELLECTUAL PROPERTY ENFORCEMENT

JUNE 2010

Table of Contents

Letter to the President of the United States and to the Congress

I am pleased to transmit the 2010 Joint Strategic Plan on Intellectual Property Enforcement.

Intellectual property laws and rights provide certainty and predictability for consumers and producers in the exchange of innovative and creative products, and for investors shifting capital to their development. Where there are insufficient resources, ability, or political will to appropriately enforce these rights, exchanges between investors, producers and consumers may be inefficient, corrupt or even dangerous.

Our entrepreneurial spirit, creativity and ingenuity are clear comparative advantages for America in the global economy. As such, Americans are global leaders in the production of creative and innovative services and products, including digital content, many of which are dependent on the protection of intellectual property rights. In order to continue to lead, succeed and prosper in the global economy, we must ensure the strong enforcement of American intellectual property rights.

The Prioritizing Resources and Organization for Intellectual Property Act (PRO-IP Act) directs the Intellectual Property Enforcement Coordinator (IPEC) to coordinate the development of a Joint Strategic Plan against counterfeiting and infringement. To prepare this Joint Strategic Plan, my office worked closely across numerous Federal agencies and departments and with significant input from the public. We heard from a broad array of Americans and received more than 1,600 public comments with specific and creative suggestions. Federal agencies, including the U.S. Departments of Agriculture (USDA), Commerce (DOC), Health and Human Services (HHS), Homeland Security (DHS), Justice (DOJ), and State (DOS), the Office of the U.S. Trade Representative (USTR) and the U.S. Copyright Office participated in the development of this Joint Strategic Plan. An appendix to this Joint Strategic Plan further details public and government input.

Through this process, we identified a number of actions the Federal government will take to enhance the protection of American intellectual property rights:

1. We will lead by example and will work to ensure that the Federal government does not purchase or use infringing products.

2. We will support transparency in the development of enforcement policy, information sharing and reporting of law enforcement activities at home and abroad.

3. We will improve coordination and thereby increase the efficiency and effectiveness of law enforcement efforts at the Federal, state and local level, of personnel stationed overseas and of the U.S. Government's international training efforts.

4. We will work with our trading partners and with international organizations to better enforce American intellectual property rights in the global economy.

5. We will secure supply chains to stem the flow of infringing products at our borders and through enhanced cooperation with the private sector.

6. We will improve data and information collection from intellectual property-related activity and continuously assess domestic and foreign laws and enforcement activities to maintain an open, fair and balanced environment for American intellectual property rightholders.

I look forward to continuing to work with you, with the Federal agencies and with the public to improve enforcement of American intellectual property rights.

Victoria A. Espinel
U.S. Intellectual Property Enforcement Coordinator

Introduction

"[W]e're going to aggressively protect our intellectual property. Our single greatest asset is the innovation and the ingenuity and creativity of the American people. It is essential to our prosperity and it will only become more so in this century."

—President Barack Obama, March 11, 2010

Americans work daily to create a better world. We create products and services that improve the world's ability to communicate, to learn, to understand diverse cultures and beliefs, to be mobile, to live better and longer lives, to produce and consume energy efficiently and to secure food, nourishment and safety. Most of the value of this work is intangible—it lies in America's entrepreneurial spirit, our creativity, ingenuity and insistence on progress and in creating a better life for our communities and for communities around the world. These intangible assets, often captured as copyrights, patents, trademarks, trade secrets and other forms of "intellectual property," reflect America's advantage in the global economy.

The U.S. Government supports strengthened enforcement of intellectual property rights for a number of reasons:

> *Growth of the U.S. economy, creation of jobs for American workers and support for U.S. exports*
>
> Enforcement of intellectual property rights is a critical and efficient tool we can use, as a government, to strengthen the economy, support jobs and promote exports. Intellectual property supports jobs across all industries, and in particular where there is a high degree of creativity, research and innovation: good jobs, with high wages and strong benefits. Intellectual property-related industries can employ an engineer working for a technology company to design the next generation of cell phones, a software developer writing a new algorithm to improve search engine results, a chemist working for a pharmaceutical company to develop a new drug, a union member helping to manufacture a newly-designed tire for automobiles, or a camera operator working on a movie set to help film the next Oscar-winning movie. Effective enforcement of intellectual property rights throughout the world will help Americans export more, grow our economy and sustain good jobs for American workers.

> *Promotion of innovation and security of America's comparative advantage in the global economy*
>
> This Administration believes strongly that promoting innovation is critical to the continued success of our nation, to addressing global challenges and to providing peace, safety and prosperity for our communities. Our ability to continue to lead as a creative, innovative and productive engine for global benefit is compromised by those countries who, for their own narrow and short-term benefit, fail to enforce the rule of law, our agreements with them or adopt policies

that create unfair markets. Americans should not face inappropriate competition from foreign companies based on advantages arising or derived from insufficient protection of intellectual property rights. Strong enforcement of intellectual property rights is an essential part of the Administration's efforts to promote innovation and ensure that the U.S. is a global leader in creative and innovative industries.

Protection of consumer trust and safety

Violations of intellectual property rights, ambiguities in law and lack of enforcement create uncertainty in the marketplace, in the legal system and undermine consumer trust. Supply chains become polluted with counterfeit goods. Consumers are uncertain about what types of behavior are appropriate and whether the goods they are buying are legal and safe. Counterfeit products can pose a significant risk to public health, such as toothpaste with dangerous amounts of diethylene glycol (a chemical used in brake fluid), military systems with untested and ineffective components to protect U.S. and allied soldiers, auto parts of unknown quality that play critical roles in securing passengers and suspect semiconductors used in life-saving defibrillators. Protecting intellectual property rights, consistent with our international obligations, ensures adherence and compliance with numerous public health and safety regulations designed to protect our communities.

National and economic security

Intellectual property infringement can undermine our national and economic security. This includes counterfeit products entering the supply chain of the U.S. military, and economic espionage and theft of trade secrets by foreign citizens and companies. The profit from intellectual property infringement is a strong lure to organized criminal enterprises, which could use infringement as a revenue source to fund their unlawful activities, including terrorism. When consumers buy infringing products, including digital content, distributed by or benefiting organized crime, they are contributing to financing their dangerous and illegal activities.

Validation of rights as protected under our Constitution

Article I, Section 8 of the U.S. Constitution vests in the Congress the discretion to establish laws to promote science and artistic creativity "by securing for limited Times to Authors and Inventors the exclusive Right to their respective Writings and Discoveries." Over the last two centuries, our Founding Fathers have been proven right. One of the reasons that the U.S. is a global leader in innovation and creativity is our early establishment of strong legal mechanisms to provide necessary economic incentives required to innovate. By the same token, fair use of intellectual property can support innovation and artistry. Strong intellectual property enforcement efforts should be focused on stopping those stealing the work of others, not those who are appropriately building upon it.

American industries that depend on intellectual property employ engineers and chemists, artists and authors, and manufacturers and laborers. As a result, anyone who invests in virtually any enterprise is also dependent on intellectual property protection. The U.S. is a global leader in developing new technologies in intellectual property-related industries. From Silicon Valley to Burbank, from Raleigh/Durham's

Research Triangle to Boston's Route 128, we lead the way in bringing new, life-changing pharmaceuticals and medical devices to consumers, developing environmentally-conscious technologies, creating innovative software products, building new communication networks and producing films, music and games craved by consumers throughout the world. However, our leadership in the development of creative and innovative products and services also makes us a global target for theft.

Combating counterfeiting and piracy requires a robust Federal response. Strong intellectual property enforcement supports American jobs, protects American ideas and invigorates our economy. Intellectual property laws provide not only legal protection for creators and consumers, but incentives to encourage investment in innovation.

Our status as a global innovation leader is compromised by those countries who fail to enforce the rule of law or international agreements, or who adopt policies that disadvantage American industries. This Administration is firmly committed to promoting innovation and protecting the creative and innovative production of the American workforce.

The Internet and other technological innovations have revolutionized society and the way we obtain information and purchase products. Lowering barriers to entry and creating global distribution channels, they have opened new markets and opportunities for American exports of information, goods and services, including enabling small and medium sized businesses to reach consumers worldwide. These innovations have also facilitated piracy and counterfeiting on a global scale. Counterfeiters have developed sophisticated distribution networks. Today, the Internet allows for a person who illegally "camcords" a film at a movie theater in Moscow to distribute a bootleg copy across the globe with the push of a button. A company in Delhi producing counterfeit pharmaceuticals can instantly create a global market. Counterfeiters in Shenzhen making routers and switches can infiltrate supply chains in the U.S.

These thieves impose substantial costs. They depress investment in technologies needed to meet global challenges. They put consumers, families and communities at risk. They unfairly devalue America's contribution, hinder our ability to grow our economy, compromise good, high-wage jobs for Americans and endanger strong and prosperous communities.

So long as the rules and rights for intellectual property are predictable and enforceable, Americans will continue to lead in the effort to improve global prosperity. There are numerous challenges to meeting these goals of predictability and enforceability. Our effort must be coordinated, efficient and comprehensive. Solutions will require strong and decisive government action, transparency and cooperation from rightholders, importers, exporters and entities that currently benefit from infringement. This Joint Strategic Plan reflects such an effort across our government, our economy and with our trading partners around the world. The 33 enforcement strategy action items spelled out in the section below represent the U.S. Government's coordinated approach to strengthening intellectual property enforcement. These action items and their implementation are our first collective step towards our goal of combating infringement.

Enforcement Strategy Action Items

As provided by the PRO-IP Act, the IPEC and the Federal agencies responsible for combating intellectual property infringement have worked together, with significant input from the public, to identify ways in which the U.S. Government can enhance intellectual property enforcement. See Appendix 1 (further describing the process). The results are the 33 enforcement strategy action items spelled out below, which will shape the coordinated fight to combat intellectual property infringement. Those action items fall within six categories of focus for the U.S.: (1) leading by example; (2) increasing transparency; (3) ensuring efficiency and coordination; (4) enforcing our rights internationally; (5) securing our supply chain; and (6) building a data-driven Government.

Leading By Example

First, the U.S. Government cannot effectively ask others to act if we will not act ourselves. To that end, the U.S. Government will lead by example and will work to ensure that the Federal government does not purchase or use infringing products.

Establishment of a U.S. Government-Wide Working Group to Prevent U.S. Government Purchase of Counterfeit Products

The U.S. Government shall establish a government-wide working group tasked with studying how to reduce the risk of the procurement of counterfeit parts by the U.S. Government. Although the Government Accountability Office (GAO) recently issued a report identifying deficiencies in the procurement process practices and policies with regard to one government agency, all government agencies would benefit from a review of such policies and practices. The IPEC will convene this working group, whose members will include the National Security Council (NSC), Department of Defense (DOD)/Acquisition, Technology and Logistics (AT&L), National Aeronautics and Space Administration (NASA), General Services Administration (GSA), DOC, Small Business Administration (SBA), DHS, and other participants as may be identified by the IPEC. The working group shall be led by the IPEC, the Administrators of GSA and Federal Procurement Policy, and the Undersecretary of Defense for AT&L at DOD. The working group shall submit to the President, within 180 days after its first meeting, a memorandum outlining its findings and issues requiring further analysis.

Use of Legal Software by Federal Contractors

Executive Order 13103, issued by President Clinton on September 30, 1998, requires that Federal agencies take steps to ensure that they use only legal copies of software. However, this prohibition on the illegal use of software does not apply equally to government contractors. The Executive Order provides for contractor certification only if the agency discovers that the contractor is using Federal funds directly to buy or maintain illegal software. To demonstrate the importance we place on the use of legal software and to set an example to our trading partners, the U.S. Government will review its practices and policies to promote the use of only legal software by contractors.

Increasing Transparency

Second, information and information sharing are critical to effective enforcement. The U.S. Government will thus support transparency in the development of enforcement policy; information sharing with, from and among federal agencies (including law enforcement agencies); and reporting of enforcement activities at home and abroad.

Improved Transparency in Intellectual Property Policy-Making and International Negotiations

The Administration supports improved transparency in intellectual property enforcement policy-making and international negotiations. As such, the U.S. Government will enhance public engagement through online outreach, stakeholder outreach, congressional consultations and soliciting feedback through advisory committees, official comment mechanisms such as *Federal Register* notices (FRN), notices of proposed rulemaking (NPRM) and notices of inquiry (NOI), as appropriate for the relevant process. In the context of trade negotiations, the Administration will pursue these objectives consistently with the approaches and considerations set out in the *President's 2010 Trade Policy Agenda*, including consideration of the need for confidentiality in international trade negotiations to facilitate the negotiation process.

Increased Information Sharing with Rightholders

As the quality of counterfeit and pirated products improves, it is becoming increasingly difficult for law enforcement officials to distinguish counterfeit or pirated goods from genuine products. Rightholders are particularly well equipped to identify the legitimacy of their own goods, through various methods, including production coding. Sharing of information between U.S. Government enforcement agencies and rightholders is therefore helpful in order to make accurate infringement determinations.

Similarly, sharing samples of circumvention devices—devices that would-be-infringers use to defeat mechanisms put in place to prevent the playing of piratical copies of copyrighted works (a modchip is a common example of a circumvention device)—would allow rightholders to assist in determining whether such devices violate an import prohibition. Furthermore, sharing of samples of, and enforcement information on, seized circumvention devices can assist rightholders in their own investigations.

The U.S. Government will take action to provide DHS components with the authority to share information and samples of goods and circumvention devices with rightholders before the government seizes the goods, so that rightholders can assist in accurate determinations of infringement and violation. The U.S. Government will also take action to provide DHS components with the authority to share samples and enforcement information related to seized circumvention devices to strengthen criminal and civil enforcement.

The U.S. Government will ensure that appropriate safeguards are implemented to protect personally identifiable information, including compliance with the Privacy Act, as warranted.

Communication with Victims/Rightholders

Infringement of intellectual property rights can happen to small businesses or other entities or people on a single occasion or, unlike some other types of crimes, it can also happen to the same victim on a repeated basis. The U.S. Government will work to help victims/rightholders understand: (1) how to report a potential intellectual property crime; (2) the types of intellectual property cases generally accepted by the U.S. Government for prosecution; and (3) the types of information that victims/rightholders should provide when referring an intellectual property case for prosecution. The U.S. Government will have ongoing communication with victims/rightholders during criminal investigations, as permitted by the Government's legal, ethical and law enforcement obligations.

Reporting on Best Practices of Our Trading Partners

Although lack of adequate enforcement remains a problem around the world, individual countries have adopted laws or practices that have led to significant improvements in intellectual property enforcement. While the U.S. needs to continue to raise concerns where they exist, we should also draw attention to progress made by other countries, including their most effective policies and successful law enforcement programs. The U.S. Government will report on progress made in other countries and note specific best practices adopted by those countries. This will serve to commend their efforts and underscore their leadership example.

Identify Foreign Pirate Websites as Part of the Special 301 Process

Included in USTR's annual Special 301 report is the Notorious Markets list, a compilation of examples of Internet and physical markets that have been the subject of enforcement action or that may merit further investigation for possible intellectual property infringements. While the list does not represent a finding of violation of law, but rather is a summary of information USTR reviewed during the Special 301 process, it serves as a useful tool to highlight certain marketplaces that deal in infringing goods and help sustain global piracy and counterfeiting.

USTR will continue to publish the Notorious Markets list as part of its annual Special 301 process. Additionally, USTR, in coordination with the IPEC, will initiate an interagency process to assess opportunities to further publicize and potentially expand on the list in an effort to increase public awareness and guide related trade enforcement actions.

Tracking and Reporting of Enforcement Activities

DOJ reports the number of prosecutions of intellectual property infringers and DHS reports the number of seizures of infringing products. In addition, under the PRO-IP Act, DOJ and the Federal Bureau of Investigation (FBI) submit annual reports to Congress detailing enforcement activities. In order to provide comprehensive information about the scope of intellectual property enforcement activities, DOJ and DHS will track and report on enforcement activities related to circumvention devices.

Sharing of Exclusion Order Enforcement Data

Under Section 337 of the Tariff Act of 1930 (19 U.S.C. § 1337), the International Trade Commission (ITC) is responsible for investigating allegations regarding unfair practices in import trade, including those related to intellectual property infringements. Once the ITC makes a determination of infringement, it issues a Section 337 exclusion order and Customs and Border Protection (CBP) bars the importation of infringing goods.

More robust information sharing between CBP and rightholders would enhance CBP's effective enforcement of exclusion orders, as well as provide transparency to rightholders. The U.S. Government will seek changes to provide CBP with the authority to share enforcement data with complainant rightholders, including denials of entry, seizures pursuant to seizure and forfeiture orders and determinations pursuant to an ITC exclusion order.

Enhanced Communications to Strengthen Section 337 Enforcement

Under Section 337 of the Tariff Act of 1930, the ITC investigates allegations regarding unfair practices in import trade, including allegations related to intellectual property infringement, as well as other forms of unfair competition. Once the ITC finds a violation of Section 337 and issues an exclusion order barring the importation of infringing goods, CBP and the ITC are responsible for determining whether imported articles fall within the scope of the exclusion order. In certain cases, this requires a determination of whether an article has been successfully redesigned to no longer infringe the right addressed in the exclusion order and therefore would no longer be denied entry. Determinations of this kind are often initiated at the request of a manufacturer, importer or other interested party and are conducted through *ex parte* procedures.

Because the parties involved in the original ITC investigation can provide useful information related to the scope of the intellectual property rights being adjudicated, any determinations subsequent to the issuance of an ITC exclusion order should involve the parties and, where appropriate, the ITC. To strengthen Section 337 as an intellectual property enforcement mechanism, the ITC and CBP will explore procedures to facilitate and encourage communications between CBP and the ITC with respect to the scope of the exclusion order. This would include current CBP-ITC communication during the investigation phase. Furthermore, CBP will consider initiatives to enhance the efficiency and transparency of the exclusion order enforcement process, including such possible solutions as the development of an inter partes proceeding that will involve relevant private parties to the ITC investigation.

Ensuring Efficiency and Coordination

Third, to increase efficiency and effectiveness and to minimize duplication and waste, the U.S. Government will strengthen the coordination of: (1) law enforcement efforts at the Federal, state and local level; (2) personnel stationed overseas; and (3) international training and capacity building efforts.

Coordination of National Law Enforcement Efforts to Avoid Duplication and Waste

Numerous Federal law enforcement agencies are charged with investigating criminal intellectual property violations. To avoid duplication and waste and to benefit from the specialized expertise of particular agencies, the IPEC will work with Federal agencies and the National Intellectual Property Rights Coordination Center (IPR Center) to ensure coordination and cooperation, including:

1. **Breadth of Cooperative Efforts:** The U.S. Government will ensure the broad participation of Federal agencies responsible for criminal intellectual property infringement investigations in cooperative efforts. To date, one of the largest cooperative efforts is the IPR Center, which was established by Immigration and Customs Enforcement (ICE). In alphabetical order, the enti-

ties that participate in the IPR Center include CBP, the Defense Criminal Investigative Service ("DCIS"), DOC International Trade Administration (ITA) and U.S. Patent and Trademark Office ("USPTO"), the FBI, the Food and Drug Administration's (FDA) Office of Criminal Investigations (OCI), GSA—Office of Inspector General, ICE, the Naval Criminal Investigative Service ("NCIS"), and the U.S. Postal Inspection Service ("USPIS"). The IPEC, in coordination with relevant Federal agencies, will work to ensure the breadth of cooperative efforts, such as those taking place at the IPR Center. As part of any such cooperative effort, law enforcement agencies will share information learned from their investigations that may aid others, such as emerging criminal trends and new infringing technologies, unless such information sharing is prohibited by law or regulation.

2. **Shared Database:** The U.S. Government will have a database—or a combination of databases serving the same function as a single database—that: (1) is shared by Federal law enforcement agencies; (2) contains information about intellectual property cases; and (3) can provide case-specific information about pending investigations, including the name and contact information for the lead investigative agent. To satisfy this requirement, the U.S. Government can use or expand existing databases, such as those used by the Organized Crime Intelligence and Operations Center (IOC-2) and the Organized Crime Drug Enforcement Task Force (OCDETF) Fusion Center, the IPR Center, or Regional Information Sharing Systems (RISS) Safe. All Federal agencies with responsibility for discovering and/or investigating intellectual property crimes will contribute their case information to the database(s). The database(s) need not include sensitive intellectual property information, such as national security information, trade secrets, or grand jury information that cannot be disclosed under Federal Rule of Criminal Procedure 6(e), nor information otherwise prohibited by law or regulation. This information sharing will assist Federal law enforcement in ensuring that appropriate resources are dedicated to investigations of the highest priority targets.

3. **De-confliction:** Federal agencies will develop protocols to determine if another agency (or another office or component of the same agency) is already investigating a matter—a process generally called de-confliction—and, where appropriate, Federal agencies will conduct joint investigations to maximize U.S. Government resources or conduct investigations by a single agency (or office or component of an agency) to minimize duplication and waste of resources. Federal agencies should use databases or clearinghouses—such as those mentioned above—to de-conflict cases.

Coordination of Federal, State and Local Law Enforcement

The U.S. Government has leveraged groups composed of Federal, state and local law enforcement to address, among other crimes, narcotics trafficking, human trafficking and terrorism. Such coordination of prosecution efforts in intellectual property crime cases will allow law enforcement to benefit from the different expertise and experiences of the various Federal agencies, of Federal, state and local law enforcement and of particular prosecutorial offices. Such coordination will also reduce duplication of resources and conflicts among Federal law enforcement agencies and between Federal and state/local law enforcement. Examples of such coordinated efforts include the 22 Federal, state and local Intellectual

Property Theft Enforcement Teams ("IPTETs") ICE recently established around the country to combat intellectual property infringement. DOJ's Bureau of Justice Assistance (BJA) has also recently funded a number of state and local intellectual property task forces that collaborate with Federal law enforcement.

To continue and expand these efforts, the Federal agencies responsible for discovering and/or investigating intellectual property crimes including, but not limited to, CBP, the FBI, and ICE will work together in local/regional working groups to coordinate their intellectual property enforcement efforts with each other and with the United States Attorneys' Offices, as appropriate, as least in localities or regions where intellectual property infringement is most prevalent. The U.S. Government will encourage state and local law enforcement and prosecutors responsible for intellectual property enforcement to participate in these working groups.

Coordination of Training for State and Local Law Enforcement and Prosecutors

The U.S. Government will provide training to interested state and local law enforcement and prosecutors on intellectual property enforcement. Federal agencies will work with each other and with state and local law enforcement organizations and non-profit entities—including the National White Collar Crime Center ("NW3C") and the National Association of Attorneys General ("NAAG")—to coordinate efforts to develop materials for such training and to provide such training.

Improve the Effectiveness of Personnel Stationed Overseas to Combat Intellectual Property Infringement

Combating intellectual property infringement overseas is a priority for the Administration because of its effect on jobs, the U.S. economy and threats to health and public safety. It is critical that we station overseas personnel in countries of concern to ensure intellectual property is made a priority. It is also critical that we ensure that overseas personnel receive clear guidance on the Administration's overall enforcement priorities. Thus, to improve the effectiveness of these personnel with regard to protecting intellectual property rights, the U.S. Government will take the following steps:

1. prioritize stationing of all overseas personnel trained to address intellectual property enforcement based on an assessment by the U.S. Government of the need to address intellectual property enforcement issues in particular countries or regions;

2. prioritize stationing of additional law enforcement personnel with significant intellectual property enforcement responsibilities overseas;

3. develop intellectual property enforcement work plans for appropriate embassy personnel to follow in all countries in which intellectual property enforcement is a priority;

4. establish or enhance working groups within embassies to implement embassy intellectual property enforcement work plans in priority countries;

5. strengthen regular coordinated communication between personnel stationed overseas and the agency headquarters to ensure U.S. government personnel stationed overseas have a clear sense of priorities and guidance; and

6. introduce and implement procedures to measure the effectiveness of overseas personnel in addressing identified intellectual property enforcement issues.

Coordination of International Capacity Building and Training

The U.S. Government has undertaken substantial efforts to reduce intellectual property infringement internationally through capacity-building exercises including seminars, workshops, outreach programs and training programs designed to educate foreign governments, citizens and private sector stakeholders on the need and mechanisms for strengthening intellectual property protection, and to provide the tools for effective enforcement of intellectual property. However, these efforts could be more effective if existing coordination was strengthened.

In order to increase coordination and to promote efficient use of U.S. Government resources, the U.S. Government will:

1. to strengthen interagency coordination of international capacity building and training, establish an interagency committee through which agencies will share plans, information and best practices and also integrate coordination of capacity building efforts with interagency coordination of overall development assistance to developing countries;

2. focus capacity building and training efforts in those countries in which intellectual property enforcement is a high priority and where those efforts can be most effective;

3. develop comprehensive needs assessments and, based on those assessments, develop agency strategic plans for capacity building in the coming years;

4. establish mechanisms to evaluate the effectiveness of capacity building and training programs;

5. deposit international intellectual property enforcement training materials or catalogs in a shared database so that all agencies have access to them to promote greater consistency and to avoid duplication and waste of resources;

6. ensure that training and capacity building materials are consistent with U.S. intellectual property laws and policy goals;

7. ensure that training offered by the U.S. Government on U.S. copyright law includes an explanation of the relevant balance provided in U.S. law between a creator's rights in his or her work and specifically defined legal limitations on those rights; and

8. coordinate training efforts with international organizations and the business community to make training more efficient.

Establishment of a Counterfeit Pharmaceutical Interagency Committee

The IPEC shall establish an interagency committee on the counterfeiting of pharmaceutical drugs and medical products. This committee will bring together the expertise of numerous Federal agencies, including the Office of National Drug Control Policy, the National Institutes of Health (NIH), DOC, DOS/U.S. Agency of International Development (USAID), HHS/FDA, the IPR Center, CBP, ICE, FBI, the Drug Enforcement Administration (DEA), USTR, and Veterans Affairs. The committee will invite experts from the private sector to participate as needed, and in full compliance with the Federal Advisory Committee Act and other relevant Federal laws and regulations. Among other issues, the committee shall examine the myriad of problems associated with unlicensed Internet pharmacies, health and safety risks in the U.S. associated with the distribution of counterfeits and the proliferation of the distribution of counterfeit pharmaceuticals in Africa. The IPEC shall chair the committee. The committee shall produce a report with specific recommendations for government action within 120 days of the commencement of its first meeting.

Enforcing Our Rights Internationally

Fourth, addressing infringement in other countries is a critical component of protecting and enforcing our rights. To that end, the U.S. Government will work collectively to strengthen enforcement of intellectual property rights internationally.

Combat Foreign-Based and Foreign-Controlled Websites that Infringe American Intellectual Property Rights

The use of foreign-based and foreign-controlled websites and web services to infringe American intellectual property rights is a growing problem that undermines our national security, particularly our national economic security. Despite the scope and increasing prevalence of such sites, enforcement is complicated because of the limits of the U.S. Government's jurisdiction and resources in foreign countries. To help better address these enforcement issues, Federal agencies, in coordination with the IPEC, will expeditiously assess current efforts to combat such sites and will develop a coordinated and comprehensive plan to address them that includes: (1) U.S. law enforcement agencies vigorously enforcing intellectual property laws; (2) U.S. diplomatic and economic agencies working with foreign governments and international organizations; and (3) the U.S. Government working with the private sector.

Enhance Foreign Law Enforcement Cooperation

International law enforcement cooperation is a critical part of combating the global nature of piracy and counterfeiting. Federal law enforcement agencies will encourage cooperation with their foreign counterparts to: (1) enhance efforts to pursue domestic investigations of foreign intellectual property infringers; (2) encourage foreign law enforcement to pursue those targets themselves; and (3) increase the number of criminal enforcement actions against intellectual property infringers in foreign countries in general. Federal law enforcement agencies will also use, as appropriate, formal cooperative agreements or arrangements with foreign governments as a tool to strengthen cross-border intellectual property enforcement efforts.

Promote Enforcement of U.S. Intellectual Property Rights through Trade Policy Tools

The U.S. Government has traditionally sought to use the tools of trade policy to seek strong intellectual property enforcement. Examples include bilateral trade dialogues and problem-solving, communicating U.S. concerns clearly through reports such as the Special 301 Report, committing our trading partners to protect American intellectual property through trade agreements such as the Anti-Counterfeiting Trade Agreement (ACTA) and the Trans-Pacific Partnership (TPP), and, when necessary, asserting our rights through the World Trade Organization (WTO) dispute settlement process. USTR, in coordination with the IPEC and relevant Federal agencies, will continue the practice of using these tools to seek robust intellectual property enforcement, including protection of patents, copyrights, trade secrets and trademarks including geographical indications, as well as strong civil, criminal and border measures. Furthermore, USTR will be vigilant in enforcing U.S. trade rights under its trade agreements. These efforts will be conducted in a manner consistent with the balance found in U.S. law and the legal traditions of U.S. trading partners.

Special 301 "Action Plans"

USTR conducts annual reviews of intellectual property protection and market access practices in foreign countries. Through an extensive Special 301 interagency process, USTR publishes a report annually, designating countries of concern on different watch lists, referred to as "priority watch list" (PWL), "watch list" and "priority foreign country." Countries placed on the PWL are the focus of increased bilateral attention concerning the problem areas. The 2010 Special 301 report countries on the PWL included Algeria, Argentina, Canada, Chile, China, India, Indonesia, Pakistan, Russia, Thailand and Venezuela.

USTR also develops action plans and similar documents to establish benchmarks, such as legislative, policy or regulatory action, and as a tool to encourage improvements by countries in order to be removed from the Special 301 list. In order to work with foreign governments to improve their practices related to intellectual property and market access, USTR, in coordination with the IPEC, will initiate an interagency process to increase the effectiveness of, and strengthen implementation of, Special 301 action plans. The action plans, or other appropriate measures, will focus on selected trading partners for which targeted efforts could produce desired results.

Strengthen Intellectual Property Enforcement through International Organizations

Numerous international organizations have an interest in and focus on intellectual property rights. The IPEC will work with relevant Federal agencies and the IPR Center to raise awareness of intellectual property enforcement and to increase international collaborative efforts through international organizations, such as the World Intellectual Property Organization (WIPO), the WTO, the World Customs Organization (WCO), the World Health Organization (WHO), the Group of Twenty Finance Ministers and Central Bank Governors (G-20), the International Criminal Police Organization (INTERPOL), the Asia-Pacific Economic Cooperation (APEC) Forum, and the Organization for Economic Co-operation and Development (OECD). By working with such organizations, the U.S. Government can strengthen international intellectual property enforcement efforts and increase cross-border diplomatic and law enforcement cooperation. In particular, the U.S. Government will explore opportunities for joint training, sharing of best practices and lessons learned and coordinated law enforcement action.

Securing Our Supply Chain

Fifth, the U.S. Government will work to secure supply chains to stem the flow of infringing products through law enforcement efforts and through enhanced cooperation with the private sector.

FDA Notification Requirement for Counterfeit Pharmaceuticals and Other Medical Products

Because of the serious risk to public health, manufacturers and importers shall be required to notify the FDA in the event of a known counterfeit of any pharmaceutical and other medical product. The required notification shall also specify any known potential adverse health consequences of the counterfeit product. Drug manufacturers shall also be required to provide the FDA with a list and complete description of any legitimate drug products that are currently being distributed in the stream of U.S. commerce on a twice annual basis, so that the FDA has updated information on all drugs and medical devices currently being sold by the manufacturer. This could be effectuated by amending 21 U.S.C. Section 331.

Mandated Use of Electronic Track and Trace for Pharmaceuticals and Medical Products

The Food, Drug and Cosmetic Act should be modified to require that manufacturers, wholesalers and dispensers implement a track-and-trace system, which allows for authentication of the product and creation of an electronic pedigree for medical products using unique identifiers for products. Effective track-and-trace systems can make it more difficult for persons to introduce counterfeit or intentionally adulterated medical products into the U.S. market, make it easier to identify persons responsible for making a product unsafe and facilitate the recall of unsafe products by more quickly identifying where a product is located in the marketplace. Privacy concerns will be considered when deciding where the information will be housed and who will have access to the information.

Increased Enforcement Efforts to Guard Against the Proliferation of Counterfeit Pharmaceuticals and Medical Devices

In an effort to further secure our supply chains, and to help stop the proliferation of counterfeit pharmaceuticals and medical devices in the stream of commerce, increased U.S. Government action is warranted. The IPEC will therefore work with relevant Federal agencies, including DHS (CBP and ICE) and HHS/FDA, to establish increased enforcement cooperation, coordination and information sharing consistent with current agreements, procedures, notices, alerts, guidance, memoranda of understanding and established partnerships for daily operations at U.S. borders. To further these efforts, the IPEC will work with these agencies to make certain that they have the enforcement authority that they need to address the problems associated with counterfeit pharmaceuticals and medical devices.

Penalty Relief for Voluntary Disclosure

In cases where importers or other parties discover that they have acquired counterfeit or pirated products without their knowledge, there is no existing process by which the importers can voluntarily disclose violations to CBP without being subject to seizures and other enforcement actions. In order to discover counterfeit goods, encourage voluntary disclosure and strengthen cooperation between industry and enforcement entities, the U.S. Government will take action to allow importers and others involved in the importation of infringing goods to receive relief from civil enforcement action as appropriate when they voluntarily disclose the violation to CBP prior to the beginning of an investigation. If a valid disclosure is made, the infringing goods in the disclosing party's possession or control would be destroyed under CBP's supervision and the disclosing party would bear the costs of destruction.

Penalize Exporters of Infringing Goods

While CBP has seizure and forfeiture authority related to the exportation of intellectual property infringing goods, it does not have express authority to issue administrative penalties on infringing exports. In order to ensure broader authority to protect U.S. intellectual property across the supply chain, the U.S. Government will seek legislative amendments to specify authority for CBP to create and implement a mechanism to evaluate and issue administrative penalties for intellectual property-related export violations.

Streamline Bonding Requirements for Circumvention Devices

One of the tools available for rightholders to assist CBP in enforcing against counterfeit and pirated goods is for rightholders to obtain a sample of the suspected product to determine if it is infringing. In those instances, CBP requires that rightholders post a bond to cover the potential loss or damage to the sample if the products are ultimately found to be non-infringing. Certain rightholders interact with CBP frequently in this cooperative manner so posting an individual transaction bond for each sample can be burdensome.

To streamline this requirement, in October 2009, CBP implemented a continuous bond option for trademark and copyright infringement cases, allowing rightholders to post a single bond that covers several transactions at different ports of entry. Contingent on CBP obtaining the authority to provide rightholders samples of circumvention devices and in order to further streamline bonding requirements, CBP will extend the new bond practice to cover samples of circumvention devices.

Facilitating Cooperation to Reduce Intellectual Property Infringement Occurring Over the Internet

The U.S. Government supports the free flow of information and freedom of expression over the Internet. An open and accessible Internet is critical to our economy. At the same time, the Internet should not be used as a means to further criminal activity. The Administration encourages cooperative efforts within the business community to reduce Internet piracy. The Administration believes that it is essential for the private sector, including content owners, Internet service providers, advertising brokers, payment processors and search engines, to work collaboratively, consistent with the antitrust laws, to address activity that has a negative economic impact and undermines U.S. businesses, and to seek practical and efficient solutions to address infringement. This should be achieved through carefully crafted and balanced agreements. Specifically, the Administration encourages actions by the private sector to effectively address repeated acts of infringement, while preserving the norms of legitimate competition, free speech, fair process and the privacy of users. While the Administration encourages cooperative efforts within the business community to reduce Internet piracy, the Administration will pursue additional solutions to the problems associated with Internet piracy, including vigorously investigating and prosecuting criminal activity, where warranted.

Establish and Implement Voluntary Protocols to Help Reduce Illegal Internet Pharmacies

Google, Yahoo and Bing recently updated voluntary protocols designed to prevent the sale of sponsored results for unlawful businesses selling counterfeit medications on-line. These protocols utilize a "White List" of pre-approved Internet pharmaceutical sellers that include verification by the National Association of Boards of Pharmacy's Verified Internet Pharmacy Practice Sites (VIPPS) or certifications from the original manufacturers of legitimate and FDA-approved pharmaceuticals. The U.S. Government applauds these efforts by the private sector and will continue to work with these companies and other search engine operators, advertising brokers and payment processors to explore methods to prohibit paid advertising for on-line illegal pharmaceutical vendors. Simultaneously, the U.S. Government will explore means by which online pharmaceutical companies operating in violation of intellectual property laws can be made subject to the full reach of law enforcement jurisdiction.

Building a Data-Driven Government

Sixth, information is critical to developing effective enforcement strategies. To that end, the U.S. Government will improve data and information collection from intellectual property-related activities and assess domestic and foreign laws and enforcement activities to enable an open and fair environment for American intellectual property rightholders.

U.S. Government Resources Spent on Intellectual Property Enforcement

Several agencies across the U.S. Government dedicate resources toward the enforcement of intellectual property. In order to better track resource baselines and inform future resource allocations dedicated to intellectual property enforcement, the IPEC will collect annually the amount of U.S. Government resources spent on intellectual property enforcement personnel, technologies, programs and other efforts.

The IPEC has already begun that process by collecting this information in Fiscal Year (FY) 2010 through a Budget Data Request (BDR), whereby agencies reported the amount of resources they dedicated to human capital and programs, identified metrics used in measuring intellectual property enforcement successes, and planned and estimated expenditures for future years. Moving forward, the IPEC will continue coordinating this BDR annually, and will request the same data and metrics to allow for cross and multi-year comparisons.

Assessing the Economic Impact of Intellectual Property-Intensive Industries

There is no known comprehensive study that attempts to measure the economic contributions of intellectual property-intensive industries across all U.S. business sectors. Improved measures of intellectual property linked with measures of economic performance would help the U.S. Government understand the role and breadth of intellectual property in the American economy and would inform policy and resource decisions related to intellectual property enforcement.

To assess the feasibility of improving measures of intellectual property and linking those measures to economic performance, the Economic and Statistics Administration (ESA) within DOC, in coordination with the IPEC, will convene an interagency meeting with relevant agencies to establish a framework for conducting this work. Once that framework is established, ESA will test the feasibility of developing improved intellectual property measures and, if those measures can be developed, they will be linked to measures of economic performance. The resulting analysis and datasets will then be made public.

Comprehensive Review of Existing Intellectual Property Laws to Determine Needed Legislative Changes

Due to changes in technology and the growing sophistication of intellectual property violators, the U.S. Government must ensure that intellectual property laws continue to effectively and comprehensively combat infringement. The IPEC will initiate and coordinate a process, working with Federal agencies, to review existing laws—whether they impose criminal and/or civil liability—to ensure that they are effectively reaching the appropriate range of infringing conduct, including any problems or gaps in scope due to changes in technologies used by infringers. Federal agencies will also review existing civil and criminal penalties to ensure that they are providing an effective deterrent to infringement (including, as to criminal penalties, reviewing the United States Sentencing Guidelines). Finally, Federal agencies will review enforcement of existing laws to determine if legislative changes are needed to enhance enforcement efforts. The initial review process will conclude within 120 days from the date of the submission of this Joint Strategic Plan to Congress. The Administration, coordinated through the IPEC, will recommend to Congress any proposed legislative changes resulting from this review process.

Supporting U.S. Businesses in Overseas Markets

With the launch of the President's National Export Initiative, it is an Administration priority to improve U.S. Government support for U.S. businesses in overseas markets. American exporters face various barriers to entry into overseas markets including barriers related to intellectual property rights. U.S. companies may be reluctant to export due to a lack of certainty that innovation, and the intellectual property rights in that innovation, can be protected. In addition, exporters may not be familiar with the legal environment in which they need to operate to protect their rights.

In coordination with the IPEC, DOC and other relevant agencies will conduct a comprehensive review of existing U.S. Government efforts to educate, guide and provide resources to those U.S. businesses that are:

1. acquiring intellectual property rights in foreign markets;

2. contemplating exporting intellectual property-based products or choosing markets for export;

3. actively entering foreign markets or facing difficulties entering foreign markets; and

4. encountering difficulties enforcing their intellectual property rights in foreign markets.

The goal of the review is to increase the scope and effectiveness of existing efforts through improved coordination of our diplomatic, cooperative, programmatic and other bilateral mechanisms. This effort will focus in particular, but not exclusively, on the Chinese market.

Summary of Enforcement Strategy Action Items

	Action Items
Leading By Example	Establishment of a U.S. Government-Wide Working Group to Prevent U.S. Government Purchase of Counterfeit Products
	Use of Legal Software by Federal Contractors
Increasing Transparency	Improved Transparency in Intellectual Property Policy-Making and International Negotiations
	Increased Information Sharing with Rightholders
	Communication with Victims/Rightholders
	Reporting on Best Practices of Our Trading Partners
	Identify Foreign Pirate Websites as Part of the Special 301 Process
	Tracking and Reporting of Enforcement Activities
	Sharing of Exclusion Order Enforcement Data
	Enhanced Communications to Strengthen Section 337 Enforcement
Ensuring Efficiency and Coordination	Coordination of National Law Enforcement Efforts to Avoid Duplication and Waste
	Coordination of Federal, State and Local Law Enforcement
	Coordination of Training for State and Local Law Enforcement and Prosecutors
	Improve the Effectiveness of Personnel Stationed Overseas to Combat Intellectual Property Infringement
	Coordination of International Capacity Building and Training
	Establishment of a Counterfeit Pharmaceutical Interagency Committee

	Action Items
Enforcing Our Rights Internationally	Combat Foreign-Based and Foreign-Controlled Websites that Infringe American Intellectual Property Rights
	Enhance Foreign Law Enforcement Cooperation
	Promote Enforcement of U.S. Intellectual Property Rights through Trade Policy Tools
	Special 301 "Action Plans"
	Strengthen Intellectual Property Enforcement through International Organizations
Securing Our Supply Chain	FDA Notification Requirement for Counterfeit Pharmaceuticals and Other Medical Products
	Mandated Use of Electronic Track and Trace for Pharmaceuticals and Medical Products
	Increased Enforcement Efforts to Guard Against the Proliferation of Counterfeit Pharmaceuticals and Medical Devices
	Penalty Relief for Voluntary Disclosure
	Penalize Exporters of Infringing Goods
	Streamline Bonding Requirements for Circumvention Devices
	Facilitating Cooperation to Reduce Intellectual Property Infringement Occurring Over the Internet
	Establish and Implement Voluntary Protocols to Help Reduce Illegal Internet Pharmacies
Building a Data-Driven Government	U.S. Government Resources Spent on Intellectual Property Enforcement
	Assessing the Economic Impact of Intellectual Property-Intensive Industries
	Comprehensive Review of Existing Intellectual Property Laws to Determine Needed Legislative Changes
	Supporting U.S. Businesses in Overseas Markets

Agencies' Intellectual Property Enforcement Missions

Department of Agriculture

USDA supports intellectual property rights enforcement related to agriculture, primarily through the provision of technical expertise in interagency trade agreement negotiations, dispute resolution and enforcement mechanisms, and through USDA's close relationships with the U.S. agricultural industry.

USDA's support to intellectual property enforcement includes the following:

- *Trade Agreements:* USDA's Foreign Agricultural Service (FAS) supports USTR in negotiating, implementation, and monitoring and enforcement of free trade agreements (FTAs), and inter-faces with U.S. agricultural industry groups on intellectual property trade agreement issues.

- *World Trade Organization:* USDA's FAS supports dispute settlement, accession processes and negotiations in the WTO related to agriculture.

- *Bilateral and Regional Dialogues and Cooperation:* USDA's FAS participates in intellectual property enforcement discussion in a wide range of trade and economic policy dialogues with trading partners, and in trade and investment framework agreement discussions. FAS Attachés overseas and staff in Washington participate in interagency working groups addressing intellectual property issues.

- *Coordination of U.S. Intellectual Property Enforcement Trade Policy:* USDA's FAS participates in the Special 301 process, an interagency venue for resolving intellectual property policy issues.

Department of Commerce

International Trade Administration

ITA strengthens the competitiveness of U.S. industry, promotes trade and investment and ensures fair trade through the rigorous enforcement of our trade laws and agreements. As part of its mission, ITA ensures that our trading partners are fulfilling their international trade commitments to enforce and protect intellectual property rights. ITA also responds to inquiries, develops trade programs and tools to help U.S. businesses and citizens enforce and protect their intellectual property rights in foreign markets, and conducts outreach to raise awareness.

The Office of Intellectual Property Rights (OIPR) is responsible for developing and coordinating ITA input on trade-related intellectual property rights policies, programs and practices and for assisting companies to overcome challenges to protecting and enforcing their intellectual property rights overseas. The U.S. Commercial Service, with offices in over 100 U.S. cities and 77 locations abroad, advocates for the interests of U.S. companies on intellectual property issues with appropriate foreign government officials, counsels U.S. companies operating or selling abroad in understanding foreign-country business climates and legal environments and assists companies to identify in-country resources to assist with registering and/or protecting their intellectual property rights through administrative or court actions.

As part of an overall strategy to educate the U.S. business community and, in particular, U.S. Small and Medium Sized Enterprises (SMEs), ITA and USPTO, working with other U.S. Government agencies and the private sector, have developed the www.StopFakes.gov/ website and a number of associated tools for small businesses. The site includes information on:

- 17 Market-Specific Toolkits, which provide detailed information on protecting U.S. intellectual property in key markets like China, Brazil and the European Union (EU).

- An online training program developed by OIPR with the Foreign Commercial Service (FCS), USPTO, and the SBA, for SMEs about evaluating, protecting and enforcing intellectual property rights (translated into Spanish and French to broaden outreach).

- A program developed by OIPR and the FCS to promote protection of intellectual property rights at domestic and international trade fairs.

- A program developed with the American Bar Association through which American SMEs can request a free, one-hour consultation with a volunteer attorney to learn how to protect and enforce their rights in Brazil, China, Egypt, India, Russia and Thailand.

- The Intellectual Property Protection and Enforcement Manual and the No Trade in Fakes Supply Chain Tool Kit, which OIPR encouraged the U.S. Chamber of Commerce and the Coalition Against Counterfeiting and Piracy (CACP) to develop and release. These documents, posted online at www.thecacp.com/, showcase proven strategies companies, both small and large, use to protect their supply chains from counterfeiters and pirates.

Patent and Trademark Office

USPTO has a long history of encouraging and supporting trading partners, particularly developing and least developed countries, to move beyond mere adoption of laws protecting intellectual property rights to the operation of effective systems for enforcement. In 1999, USPTO expanded its technical assistance and capacity building activities to address intellectual property enforcement. Such capacity building has included training for foreign government law enforcement officials, prosecutors, the judiciary and customs and border enforcement officials, and technical assistance on drafting laws and regulations on enforcement-related issues.

USPTO has created a flexible team enterprise that meets the challenges of intellectual property enforcement in today's global economy by: (1) carrying out statutory and international treaty obligations to assist developing nations in implementing accessible and effective intellectual property enforcement systems; (2) responding rapidly to changing global and international conditions; (3) establishing alliances with other national and international intellectual property organizations to strengthen, protect and enforce American intellectual property rights globally; and (4) working with other U.S. Government agencies, national intellectual property enforcement authorities and international organizations to increase the accessibility, efficiency and effectiveness of civil, administrative and criminal enforcement mechanisms in global trade, foreign markets and electronic commerce.

USPTO regularly consults with foreign governments and other U.S. Government agencies on the substantive, technical aspects of intellectual property enforcement laws, legal and judicial regimes, civil and criminal procedures, border measures and administrative regulations relating to enforcement; advises USTR and DOC on the trade-related aspects of intellectual property enforcement and serves as technical advisors on enforcement provisions in trade agreements by reviewing, analyzing and monitoring legislative and legal developments pertaining to intellectual property enforcement mechanisms, administration and public education efforts; develops, conducts, coordinates and participates in training programs, conferences and seminars, and develops training materials, including long-distance learning modules, to improve the level of expertise of those responsible for intellectual property enforcement and the overall enforcement environment; gathers information on and monitors foreign national enforcement systems, and coordinates intellectual property enforcement-related activities undertaken by various intergovernmental and non-governmental organizations; and provides technical expertise on legislation involving intellectual property enforcement.

USPTO's Global Intellectual Property Academy, established in 2006, is a focal point for intellectual property rights technical assistance and training, and a crucial component in an integrated approach to enforcement training and capacity-building, both domestically and internationally. In addition, USPTO operates the overseas intellectual property Attaché program, which places resident experts in a number of U.S. missions abroad in order to provide direct, on-the-ground technical expertise, support and coordination of all intellectual property rights protection and enforcement issues, including training and capacity-building activities for foreign government officials.

Commercial Law Development Program

The Commercial Law Development Program (CLDP) improves the legal environment for U.S. businesses worldwide by removing non-tariff barriers to trade and ensuring effective implementation of intellectual property policies and enforcement provisions. CLDP programs level the playing field for U.S. industries to compete in developing markets and provide follow-up support to countries that have limited capacity to implement some provisions of trade agreements entered into with the U.S. Although CLDP technical assistance is largely government-to-government, each program is designed to address a pressing need identified by both local and U.S. businesses.

CLDP partners with other offices within DOC (including USPTO, ITA and National Telecommunications and Information Administration (NTIA)), as well as DHS, DOJ, DOS/ USAID to provide capacity building and enforcement technical assistance in developing countries. CLDP's intellectual property work with host countries covers drafting legislation, establishing regulations, increasing skills development, promoting public outreach and ensuring transparency. Many programs address needs across regions by gathering judiciaries, policy-makers and regulators from multiple countries to share best practices and develop workable solutions to regional problems related to counterfeiting and piracy. CLDP's intellectual property work over the years has led to the development of a small library of case studies in a multitude of languages that include technology transfer, licensing and border measures. These materials, frequently shared with other U.S. Government partners, are essential learning tools for developing countries looking to improve intellectual property enforcement.

More information about CLDP's work and successes related to intellectual property enforcement and capacity building can be found at www.cldp.doc.gov.

Department of Health and Human Services | Food and Drug Administration

The FDA is responsible for protecting the public health by assuring the safety and efficacy of medical products, and the safety of foods. Expanded markets and more complex supply chains have required the FDA to find new ways to safeguard global public health. The FDA is acutely aware of the illegality of and the direct-and-indirect risk posed to the public health by counterfeit medical products, infant formula and foods that falsely represent their identity and/or source. Those who manufacture and distribute falsified medical products and foods not only defraud patients and consumers, they also deny ill patients the medical products that can alleviate suffering and save lives and, for a formula that may be an infant's sole source of nutrition, the healthy start in life that every child needs. Consequently, the FDA takes all reports of suspect counterfeits seriously and the FDA's regulatory officials have responded to this emerging threat by: strengthening its ability to prevent the introduction of falsified medical products and foods into the U.S. distribution chain, facilitating the identification of falsified medical products and foods, and by minimizing the risk and exposure of patients and consumers to falsified products through recalls, public awareness campaigns and other steps.

As a part of these efforts, the FDA's OCI expeditiously investigates reports of suspected falsified products in order to protect U.S. citizens. Specifically, OCI investigates counterfeit products that violate 18 U.S.C. Section 2320 and 21 U.S.C. Section 331(i). OCI routinely coordinates counterfeit investigations and intelligence with other international, Federal, state and local law enforcement agencies and has initiated numerous investigations focused on protecting the public health that have led to criminal convictions.

The issue of falsified medical products and food is a global issue that requires a global solution and the FDA is working with its international regulatory partners to address the public health aspects of counterfeit medical products and foods. The FDA has also worked with our partners in foreign markets to strategically establish FDA offices worldwide that help provide technical assistance, among other things, to help countries enhance their regulatory systems to ensure that counterfeits are kept out of the legitimate supply chain so consumers receive safe, effective and quality products. In addition, the FDA is also working with U.S. medical product supply chain stakeholders to put measures in place in the U.S. to ensure the integrity of the U.S. closed distribution system, such as the tracking and tracing of prescription drugs, in order to keep counterfeits out of this system.

Department of Homeland Security

DHS plays a key role in the protection of intellectual property rights. In the pursuit of an effective intellectual property enforcement strategy, DHS aims to ensure the facilitation of legitimate trade, while enforcing U.S. trade and intellectual property rights laws, as well as investigating intellectual property rights violations, specifically trademark, counterfeiting and copyright piracy. In February 2010, DHS presented the Quadrennial Homeland Security Review (QHSR) to Congress, which outlines a strategic framework for DHS' mission. Intellectual property rights enforcement falls within Mission 2 of the QHSR, which identifies the safeguarding of lawful trade and travel as one if its key goals. DHS is able to execute its mission through its components, including CBP, ICE, U.S. Secret Service (USSS) and others.

DHS actively engages with international organizations like the WCO and INTERPOL; works to develop increased information sharing and partnership programs involving trade; actively participates in global intellectual property rights training; and works with other U.S. Government agencies to further build and enhance intellectual property rights efforts. DHS components continue to work toward enhancing its intellectual property enforcement capabilities within its agency-wide mission to secure the nation and to facilitate the secure flow of legitimate goods through legitimate trade and travel.

DHS conducts several joint operations to investigate and act against intellectual property violations. For example, Operation Guardian is a DHS-led, multi-agency public health and safety initiative, conducted with ICE, CBP, FDA, the Consumer Product Safety Commission (CPSC), USPIS, USDA, and the Government of Mexico's Tax Administration Service. Since Operation Guardian's inception in FY 2008, ICE has initiated 437 investigations which have resulted in 102 criminal arrests, 25 administrative arrests, 155 search warrants and, with CBP, 925 seizures valued at over $26 million. Further, Operation Apothecary is another DHS-led multi-agency operation, conducted with ICE, CBP, FDA and USPIS that identified vulnerabilities in the mail and express courier entry process that allowed for the smuggling of commercial quantities of counterfeit, unapproved and/or adulterated drugs. Since Operation Apothecary's inception, ICE has initiated 274 investigations which have resulted in 87 criminal arrests, 58 search warrants and, with CBP, 664 seizures valued at over $2.7 million.

Customs and Border Protection

As the Federal agency responsible for the management, control and protection of U.S. borders, CBP is critical to enforcement of intellectual property rights. CBP acts under its own authorities to seize and forfeit goods that infringe on trademarks, trade names and copyrights; conduct audits; and impose and collect fines and penalties against intellectual property infringement. CBP also enforces exclusion and seizure and forfeiture orders issued by the ITC for imports that are determined to be intellectual property rights infringing. CBP is implementing a 5-year strategy for intellectual property enforcement to ensure the competitiveness of America's businesses, prevent harm to consumer health and safety and protect our way of life against threats to critical infrastructure and national security posed by the theft of intellectual property. CBP has laid out a number of initiatives, including private sector partnership programs to facilitate legitimate trade, enhanced targeting and training to increase interdictions of intellectual property infringing goods and levying penalties and conducting audits more effectively to deter intellectual property violations. CBP's 5-year strategy leverages resources and partnerships with U.S. industry, other Federal agencies and foreign governments in a comprehensive plan to attack intellectual property rights infringement throughout the international trade process. CBP receives allegations of illegal importation through its on-line e-allegations website at http://www.cbp.gov/xp/cgov/trade/trade_programs/e_allegations/. Allegations of trade violations may also be reported by calling 1-800-BE-ALERT.

Immigration and Customs Enforcement

ICE is a lead U.S. agency for the investigation of criminal intellectual property violations involving the illegal production, smuggling, and distribution of counterfeit and pirated products, as well as associated money laundering violations. ICE seizes for forfeiture goods associated with these investigations, such as those that infringe on trademarks, trade names, and copyrights. ICE criminal investigations focus on identifying, disrupting and dismantling the transnational criminal organizations that promulgate this activity. In addition to the 26 Special Agent in Charge offices responsible for conducting domestic enforcement actions, ICE has 63 Attaché Offices in 44 countries that coordinate with host governments to conduct intellectual property enforcement that extend beyond U.S. borders.

IPR Center

To more effectively counter the flood of infringing products, ICE established the IPR Center. The mission of the IPR Center is to address and combat predatory and unfair trade practices that threaten our economic stability and national security, restrict the competitiveness of U.S. industry in world markets, and place the public's health and safety at risk. The IPR Center brings together key domestic and foreign investigative agencies and industry partners to increase the efficient and effective leverage of resources, skills and authorities to provide a comprehensive response. The IPR Center maintains an intellectual property theft reporting system through its website at www.ICE.gov, through email at IPRCenter@dhs.gov and through a toll free phone number at 866-IPR-2060.

U.S. Secret Service

USSS investigates violations of laws relating to counterfeiting of obligations and securities of the U.S.; financial crimes that include, but are not limited to, access device fraud, financial institution fraud, identity theft, computer fraud; and computer-based attacks on our nation's financial, banking and telecommunications and critical infrastructure. As part of the investigative mission of safeguarding the nation's financial infrastructure, USSS investigations discover links to intellectual property violations. In response to the growing problem of intellectual property theft, USSS, through its Electronic Crimes Task Force (ECTF) program will continue to support Federal, state and local law enforcement agencies and prosecutors to combat computer and intellectual property crime and promote information sharing between government and the private industry.

Department of Justice

Aggressive enforcement of intellectual property laws is a high priority of DOJ. DOJ combats intellectual property theft and related intellectual property crime utilizing the full resources of its Criminal Division, U.S. Attorneys' Offices and Civil Division, as well as the investigatory and law enforcement resources of the FBI and other law enforcement partner agencies. DOJ's intellectual property priorities include the investigation and prosecution of intellectual property crimes involving: (1) health and safety; (2) trade secrets and economic espionage; and (3) commercial on-line piracy and counterfeiting. In addition, DOJ affirmatively supports the intellectual property enforcement efforts of its state and local partners through the use of targeted intellectual property-focused grant programs.

Criminal Division and U.S. Attorneys' Offices

DOJ prosecutes the most serious perpetrators of intellectual property crimes involving a wide range of criminal offenses. Since 1999, when then-Deputy Attorney General Holder announced DOJ's first intellectual property enforcement initiative, the Criminal Division has dramatically increased its intellectual property focus, resulting in an 800% increase in the number of intellectual property investigations and prosecutions. DOJ's intellectual property prosecution mission is handled by the 94 U.S. Attorneys' Offices and the Criminal Division's Computer Crime and Intellectual Property Section (CCIPS).

Intellectual property prosecutions through DOJ's 94 U.S. Attorneys' Offices utilize the knowledge and skills of highly specialized Assistant U.S. Attorneys working under its Computer Hacking and Intellectual Property (CHIP) coordinator program. The program consists of a network of over 220 specially-trained Federal prosecutors in U.S. Attorneys' Offices across the country who aggressively pursue computer crime and intellectual property offenses. Each U.S. Attorney's Office has at least one CHIP prosecutor; in addition, 25 U.S. Attorneys' Offices have CHIP Units, which consist of two to eight CHIP attorneys each. Each CHIP prosecutor has four core responsibilities to: (1) prosecute computer crime and intellectual property offenses; (2) serve as the district's legal counsel on matters relating to those offenses, and the collection of electronic or digital evidence; (3) train prosecutors and law enforcement personnel in the region; and (4) conduct public and industry outreach and awareness. Most CHIP prosecutors also work on other non-intellectual property cases, depending on the needs of their respective districts.

DOJ's CHIP program is complemented by the Criminal Division's CCIPS, a highly specialized team of 40 prosecutors focused on computer crime and intellectual property offenses. Fourteen CCIPS attorneys are devoted exclusively to the intellectual property criminal enforcement program. These attorneys prosecute intellectual property cases; assist in developing and implementing DOJ's criminal intellectual property enforcement strategy and legislative and policy initiatives; provide advice and guidance to agents and prosecutors in the field on a 24-hour basis; develop training and resource materials for prosecutors and investigative agents both domestically and abroad; work with Federal agency partners to strengthen overall U.S. intellectual property enforcement efforts; and provide public outreach and training to intellectual property creators, owners and industry.

The cornerstone of DOJ's strategy to strengthen international intellectual property criminal enforcement is the Intellectual Property Law Enforcement Coordinator (IPLEC) program. With support from DOS, DOJ has deployed two experienced Federal prosecutors to serve as IPLECs in Bangkok, Thailand for Southeast Asia, and in Sofia, Bulgaria for Eastern Europe. The IPLECs provide operational assistance and critical intellectual property training to increase in-country enforcement capacity. In addition, in the past five years, DOJ attorneys have provided training and education on intellectual property enforcement to over 10,000 prosecutors, police, judicial officers and other government officials from over 100 countries.

DOJ has also incorporated intellectual property into its existing International Organized Crime Strategy and has assigned a prosecutor to serve as Counsel to the IOC-2. DOJ's Criminal Division, the FBI, DHS, and other relevant participating Federal agencies are coordinating their efforts through IOC-2 and working to ensure that critical intellectual property-related intelligence and case information is contributed to its data pool.

Civil Division

Intellectual property enforcement is also an integral part of the mission of three sections of the Department's Civil Division: the Intellectual Property Section, the National Courts Section and the Office of Consumer Litigation. Through the Civil Division's Intellectual Property Section, DOJ assists with prosecution of civil actions to recover penalties imposed by CBP with respect to the importation of counterfeit goods, brings affirmative cases when U.S. intellectual property is infringed, and consults with other sections of DOJ and other agencies on intellectual property matters. The National Courts Section prosecutes civil actions to recover various penalties or customs duties arising out of negligent or fraudulent import transactions, many of which include importation of counterfeit goods. The National Courts Section also defends CBP enforcement of the ITC's Section 337 exclusion orders at the Court of International Trade; these orders are an important tool for intellectual property enforcement. Finally, the Office of Consumer Litigation enforces and defends the consumer protection statutes of the FDA, including the criminal provisions of the Food, Drug, and Cosmetics Act that govern counterfeit drugs and medical devices.

Federal Bureau of Investigation

The FBI's strategic objective is to disrupt and dismantle state sponsored groups and international and domestic criminal organizations that steal, manufacture, distribute and otherwise profit from the theft of intellectual property. The highest priorities for intellectual property rights investigations are counterfeit health and safety products and theft of trade secrets. The FBI aggressively pursues intellectual property enforcement through liaison with private industry, domestic and foreign law enforcement partners and its partnership with the IPR Center. The FBI's Intellectual Property Rights Unit (IPRU) became fully operational within the IPR Center on April 15, 2010, and now includes five dedicated FBI agents who work full time at the Center. In addition, by the end of FY 2010, the FBI intends to employ over 50 Special Agents exclusively devoted to pursuing intellectual property investigations operating in field offices throughout the country and four enhanced intellectual property squads.

Additionally, the FBI's IPRU is fully engaged with other FBI divisions, including the Criminal Investigative Division and Organized Crime and Health Care Fraud Units, as well as the Counterintelligence Division Economic Espionage Unit, to coordinate and track theft of trade secret investigations that have a state sponsorship nexus. The objective of the FBI's Counterintelligence Division's Economic Espionage Program is to prevent the loss of trade secrets to foreign agents, governments and instrumentalities as defined by the Economic Espionage Act of 1996. These collaborations act as a force multiplier allowing for multiple criminal charges resulting in higher penalties for offenders.

The FBI also established an Intelligence Fusion Group at the IPR Center. Together the partner agencies define the intellectual property rights threat picture, share tactical and strategic intelligence, establish IPR Center joint collection requirements, produce joint intelligence products and develop the national strategy.

The FBI also trains domestic and international law enforcement officials in intellectual property rights matters. The FBI is collaborating with its partner agencies to develop more comprehensive and advanced intellectual property training curriculum. The curriculum will ensure a uniform foundation across law enforcement agencies conducting intellectual property rights investigations and provide state and local law enforcement and industry liaisons with information as to how to most effectively partner with the Federal government on intellectual property rights investigations.

Office of Justice Programs

DOJ affirmatively supports the intellectual property enforcement efforts of its state and local law enforcement partners through grants awarded by its Office of Justice Programs, BJA. In 2009, BJA created the Intellectual Property Enforcement, Training, and Technical Assistance Program consisting of eight field-initiated grants and two training and technical assistance grants. The program is designed to provide national support and improve the capacity of state and local criminal justice systems to address criminal intellectual property enforcement, including prosecution, prevention, training and technical assistance. BJA also formed a partnership with the NW3C and NAAG to improve the quantity and quality of enforcement and prosecution of intellectual property crimes by providing training and technical assistance to state and local officials.

Department of Justice Task Force on Intellectual Property

Overseeing and coordinating all of DOJ's intellectual property enforcement efforts is the newly revitalized DOJ Task Force on Intellectual Property. This Task Force, which is chaired by the Deputy Attorney General, is composed of senior officials from the offices of the Attorney General, the Deputy Attorney General, and the Associate Attorney General, the Criminal Division, the Civil Division, the Antitrust Division, the Office of Legal Policy, the Office of Justice Programs, the Attorney General's Advisory Committee, the Executive Office for U.S. Attorneys and the FBI. The Task Force monitors and coordinates overall intellectual property enforcement efforts at DOJ, provides a vehicle for increased cooperation with Federal, state and local law enforcement and serves as an engine of policy development to comprehensively address the evolving technological and legal landscape of intellectual property crimes.

Department of State

Protecting American intellectual property abroad is a DOS priority and DOS works closely with other U.S. government agencies, the private sector and foreign governments to combat piracy and counterfeiting. U.S. embassies, consulates and missions are on the front line of protecting U.S. intellectual property rights: responding to complaints raised by U.S. companies and vigorously pressing foreign governments to fulfill their bilateral and international obligations. In addition to diplomatic resources, DOS uses training and public diplomacy strategies to support these goals.

Robert D. Hormats, DOS Undersecretary for Economic, Energy, and Agricultural Affairs, is the senior economic official at the DOS. He advises the Secretary of State on international economic policy, including intellectual property issues, and serves as the U.S. government's Sous-Sherpa for the G8/G20 process. DOS' Office of International Intellectual Property Enforcement (IPE), in the Bureau of Economic, Energy, and Business Affairs (EEB), was founded by Congress in 2005, and is dedicated specifically to promoting intellectual property enforcement and innovation. The IPE team works with officers at DOS' overseas posts and regional bureaus to ensure that the interests of American rightholders are represented overseas, and to highlight the integral role of intellectual property rights protection in the development of the global economy. IPE works with other U.S. Government agencies in international organizations and bilateral negotiations dedicated to intellectual property enforcement, including the WIPO and the WTO/ Trade-Related Aspects of Intellectual Property Rights (TRIPS) Council.

EEB and State's Bureau of International Narcotics and Law Enforcement together implement a Congressionally-earmarked $4 million/year intellectual property enforcement training and technical assistance for developing countries that funds an average of ten projects per year. DOS' public diplomacy programs include a group international visitor program sponsored by the Bureau of Educational and Cultural Affairs that invites up to 30 foreign intellectual property stakeholders for three weeks of capacity-building meetings and observations in the U.S.

Executive Office of the President | United States Trade Representative

USTR is supporting and implementing President Obama's commitment to aggressively protect American intellectual property internationally. As the President said just a few months ago,

"Our single greatest asset is the innovation and the ingenuity and creativity of the American people. It is essential to our prosperity and it will only become more so in this century."

The President spoke of the importance of making sure that American businesses are paid appropriately and intellectual property is not stolen. He related this to our work at USTR:

"That's why USTR is using the full arsenal of tools available to crack down on practices that blatantly harm our businesses, and that includes negotiating proper protections and enforcing our existing agreements, and moving forward on new agreements, including the proposed Anti-Counterfeiting Trade Agreement."

The ACTA, mentioned by President Obama, is an initiative to negotiate a new intellectual property enforcement agreement with a number of key trading partners who share our ambition and commitment to stepping up the fight against global counterfeiting and piracy.

Other key tools that USTR uses to advance the cause of intellectual property rights enforcement include:

- *Trade Agreements:* USTR works with countries to strengthen their intellectual property enforcement regimes through trade agreements. The ACTA negotiations are one example. Another is the negotiation, implementation, monitoring and enforcement of U.S. FTAs that include world-class provisions on intellectual property rights enforcement.

- *World Trade Organization:* This multilateral organization provides opportunities for USTR to lead engagement with trading partners on intellectual property enforcement issues in several contexts, including accession processes for prospective members like Russia, the Council for TRIPS and dispute settlement.

- *Special 301 and preference program reviews:* USTR uses the "Special 301" process to encourage specific trading partners to address significant deficiencies in intellectual property protection, including weak intellectual property enforcement. Each April, USTR issues a Special 301

Report setting out specific intellectual property rights concerns in countries worldwide. USTR works with other countries in other contexts, such as reviews under the Generalized System of Preferences (GSP) and other trade preference programs to ensure that the country is making progress on providing adequate and effective protection and enforcement of intellectual property rights.

- *Bilateral and Regional Dialogues and Cooperation:* USTR leads or is a significant participant in intellectual property enforcement discussion in a wide range of other trade and economic policy dialogues with trading partners. A few of the many examples include the APEC Forum; the U.S.-China Strategic and Economic Dialogue; the U.S.-China Joint Commission on Commerce and Trade; the U.S.-EU Summit; and the U.S.-Russia Intellectual Property Rights Working Group. Intellectual property rights issues also feature prominently in many of our Trade and Investment Framework Agreement discussions.

- *Coordination of U.S. Intellectual Property Rights Enforcement Trade Policy:* USTR leads the interagency trade policy coordination process, including on intellectual property rights, pursuant to statute and Executive Orders. USTR consults regularly with stakeholders, including through numerous advisory committees. USTR provides trade policy leadership and expertise across the full range of interagency initiatives on intellectual property rights and innovation policy, including intellectual property enforcement matters.

The Library of Congress | The Copyright Office

The Copyright Office advises Congress on national and international issues relating to copyright and provides information and assistance to Federal departments and agencies and the Judiciary on national and international issues relating to copyright. *See* 17 U.S.C. §701.

The Copyright Office does not have enforcement duties, but supports the copyright enforcement activities of the U.S. Government in a number of ways.

Regarding international matters, the Office plays a substantive role on the U.S. delegations to international organizations such as WIPO, working with USPTO and other interested agencies to establish and implement U.S. copyright initiatives. Copyright issues also frequently arise in the context of trade, in which the Copyright Office works very closely with the USTR and other agencies to address copyright enforcement deficiencies in legal systems of our trading partners.

The Copyright Office always contributes to the Special 301 process and 2010 was no exception. This year, the Office's contribution included detailing an attorney from the Office of Policy and International Affairs to USTR to be the Special 301 Coordinator. In addition, the Copyright Office has lent its technical expertise to USTR's premier enforcement-related initiative, ACTA.

The Copyright Office also engages in training, education and outreach programs. For example, in cooperation with WIPO, the Copyright Office hosted a week-long training program entitled, "International Training for Developing Countries and Countries in Transition on Emerging Issues in Copyright and Related Rights and Issues Pertaining to Blind and Visually Impaired Persons." The program ran from March 8 to March 12 and featured several panels and speakers devoted to subjects related to copyright enforcement. Participation in the enforcement section of the program involved speakers from across the U.S. Government, including Ms. Victoria Espinel, the IPEC, and Ms. Kira Alvarez, USTR's Chief Negotiator for Intellectual Property Enforcement, as well as the Copyright Office and speakers representing a wide array of stakeholders.

On April 21, 2010, the Copyright Office co-sponsored the "Internet Intermediary/Joint Liability Roundtable" in Beijing, China along with USPTO, the National Copyright Administration of China, and China's Ministry of Commerce. This event brought together Chinese copyright and trade officials, judges and academics with U.S. copyright and trade officials and stakeholders for a frank and candid exchange of copyright enforcement on the Internet.

Agencies' 2010 Major Intellectual Property Enforcement Activities to Date

Department of Agriculture

USDA's intellectual property enforcement-related activities include:

- *Trade Agreements:* USDA's FAS supports USTR in negotiating, implementation, and monitoring and enforcement of FTAs, and interfaces with U.S. agricultural industry groups on intellectual property trade agreement issues.

- *World Trade Organization:* USDA's FAS supports dispute settlement, accession processes and negotiations in the WTO related to agriculture.

- *Bilateral and Regional Dialogues and Cooperation:* USDA's FAS participates in intellectual property enforcement discussion in a wide range of trade and economic policy dialogues with trading partners, and in trade and investment framework agreement discussions. FAS Attachés overseas and staff in Washington participate in interagency working groups addressing intellectual property issues.

- *Coordination of U.S. Intellectual Property Enforcement Trade Policy:* USDA's FAS participates in the Special 301 process, an interagency venue for resolving intellectual property policy issues.

Department of Commerce

International Trade Administration

- *Trade Agreements Compliance and Market Access:* OIPR monitors foreign governments' implementation of and compliance with international trade agreements. As part of that work, OIPR assists U.S. rightholders overcome specific barriers in foreign markets that impede commercial transactions involving U.S. intellectual property. Since January 1, 2010, OIPR has initiated 21 market access and compliance cases in 13 different foreign markets on behalf of U.S. rightholders. Of those 21 cases, 18 were on behalf of U.S. SMEs.

- *Translation of SME Training Module to French and Spanish:* In April 2010, OIPR launched the French and Spanish versions of its online SME training module, which help firms recognize, register and enforce their intellectual property rights. This step increases access to this important resource.

- *OIPR Participates in the Mexico and New Zealand Rounds of the ACTA Negotiation:* In January and April 2010, OIPR staff represented the ITA on the U.S. negotiating team during the Mexico and New Zealand rounds for the ACTA negotiations.

- *ITA Hosts a Meeting of the Trans-Atlantic Consumer Dialogue on ACTA:* In April 2010, OIPR staff hosted and participated in a day-long meeting of the Trans-Atlantic Consumer Dialogue in which both U.S. and European consumer groups discussed the ACTA negotiation.

- *Croatia Intellectual Property Right Tool Kit:* The U.S. Commercial Service in Zagreb, Croatia, in close cooperation with OIPR and USPTO, developed the Croatia Intellectual Property Rights Toolkit to aid U.S. rightholders in Croatia. This toolkit has been posted on the website of the U.S. Embassy in Zagreb, Croatia, and can also be accessed through a link from www.StopFakes.gov/.

- *2010 Special 301 Report:* ITA played a significant role during the interagency review led by USTR in the lead up to the 2010 Special 301 Report's publication on April 30, 2010. ITA coordinated six industry meetings for DOC staff, and actively participated in all interagency discussions.

- *U.S.-EU Intellectual Property Rights Working Group:* On June 7, 2010, ITA co-chaired a meeting of the U.S.-EU Intellectual Property Rights Working Group in Brussels, Belgium. At the meeting, ITA and other U.S. Government agencies held detailed discussions with the European Commission on U.S.-EU cooperative efforts to strengthen intellectual property rights enforcement and protection in key third-country. ITA also held talks with DG Enterprise on ways in which the U.S. and EU can leverage resources to help SMEs.

Patent and Trademark Office

- USPTO has participated in the ACTA negotiations, including the recent rounds in Mexico (January 2010), New Zealand (April 2010), and Switzerland (June 2010).

- In March 2010, USPTO organized an intellectual property border enforcement workshop in Cairo, Egypt, to support efforts by the government of Egypt in revamping its customs laws.

- In March 2010, USPTO conducted a regional workshop in Estonia, for investigators and prosecutors on investigation and prosecution of digital piracy for officials from Estonia, Latvia, Lithuania and Russia, with officials from Sweden and Finland also participating.

- In March 2010, USPTO organized a regional seminar on combating counterfeit products for the East African Community in Dar Es Salaam, Tanzania, with the seminar timed to capitalize on progress the East African Community has made in developing an anti-counterfeiting policy statement and an anti-counterfeiting law.

- In March 2010, USPTO participated in the APEC-IPEG 30th meeting in Hiroshima, Japan, at which, USPTO led the U.S. delegation at the meeting and continued to push initiatives on anti-camcording and signal piracy, as well as trade in counterfeit goods.

- As part of a partnership with INTERPOL and the WCO, USPTO co-funded Operation Jupiter trainings in Paraguay (April 2010), Peru (May 2010), and Western Africa (May 2010), with these regional activities focused on transnational criminal organizations involved in intellectual property crime.

- USPTO, as part of its on-going partnership with the Association of Southeast Asian Nations (ASEAN), organized and funded intellectual property rights enforcement capacity-building programs for regional customs officials in Brunei, Darussalam (March 2010), and public prosecutors and law enforcement officials/police in Cambodia (May 2010).

- In May 2010, USPTO organized a two-week study tour program for Mexican judges in the U.S., and will provide a detail to the Embassy in Mexico City to work on intellectual property enforcement and protection-related programs from June to September 2010.

- USPTO has provided expert technical advice to USTR in the TPP Agreement negotiations on enforcement-related provisions.

Commercial Law Development Program

- In March 2010, CLDP held a U.S. Consultations on Intellectual Property and Technology Transfer for a group of Algerian representatives from the GAO and the private sector.

- CLDP held a follow up workshop in March 2010 for representatives of Kosovo's information technology industry on intellectual property and software licensing.

- In April 2010, in collaboration with DHS and DOJ, CLDP held a two-day training consultation on intellectual property enforcement at the borders for 150 participants from the Malian Customs Service as well as regional delegations from Cameroon, Cote d'Ivoire, Togo, Benin, Burkina Faso and Senegal, in Bamako.

- In April 2010, as a part of ongoing judicial capacity building programs in Libya, CLDP arranged consultations and training with DOJ enforcement attorneys, and USPTO enforcement attorneys for four high-level Justice Officials from Libya.

- In May 2010, CLDP held a three-day workshop in Accra for 50 participants that facilitated the development of an Interagency Intellectual Property Task Force, by bringing together a wide range of Ghanaian agencies and stakeholders involved in the fight against counterfeiting and piracy.

- In May 2010, as part of the AGCI program, CLDP held a regional workshop on the adjudication of intellectual property cases in collaboration with USPTO and DOJ and the Southern African Development Community (SADC) for a group of judges from across the SADC region to Botswana.

- In May and June 2010, CLDP implemented a two-part program in Pakistan focusing on intellectual property. Part one helped create a core group of specialists able to advise tenants of university technology incubators and to manage university technology transfer offices. Part two built the information technology community's capacity to manage intellectual capital, and support its efforts to modify the legislative and institutional environment (focus on copyright registration).

- In June 2010, CLDP held a program in Ukraine for 65 customs officials and other government authorities of Ukraine, Poland, Slovakia, Hungary, Romania, Moldova and Russia on ways to better interdict the entry of infringing goods.

Department of Health and Human Services | Food and Drug Administration

- In January 2010, HHS/FDA issued a public warning about a counterfeit version of the weight-loss drug Alli 60 mg capsules (120 count refill pack) being sold over the Internet, which included an incorrect active ingredient that should not be used without a prescription and could be harmful to certain patients.

- In March 2010, the FDA issued a standard for unique identification for packages of prescription drugs, which is an important first step towards establishing track and trace and supply chain security in the U.S.

- In March 2010, the FDA warned health care providers and consumers about counterfeit surgical mesh being distributed in the U.S. under the C. R. Bard/Davol brand name. Surgical mesh products are used to reinforce soft tissue where weakness exists.

- In May 2010, the FDA was actively engaged in discussions at the World Health Assembly, seeking international consensus on public health strategies to address the problem of counterfeit medical products.

- Throughout 2010, the FDA and CBP are conducting drug inspection "blitzes" to identify counterfeit and substandard drugs sent to U.S. consumers usually as a result of purchases over the Internet.

Department of Homeland Security

DHS has conducted a number of intellectual property rights enforcement activities in 2010.

- *QHSR:* In February 2010, DHS presented the QHSR to Congress, which identified the safeguarding of lawful trade and travel as one if its key goals.

- *Anti-Counterfeiting Trade Agreement:* DHS, including CBP and the Office of Policy, served as subject matter experts advising the USTR at the Mexico negotiating round in January, and CBP, ICE, and the Office of Policy attended the New Zealand negotiating rounds in April.

- *2010 Special 301 Report:* DHS provided significant input and subject matter expertise to the interagency review led by USTR to publish the 2010 Special 301 Report on April 30, 2010.

Customs and Border Protection

- *5-Year Strategy for Intellectual Property Rights Enforcement:* In early July, CBP will unveil an ambitious and comprehensive 5-year strategy for intellectual property enforcement aimed at improving enforcement throughout the entire international trade process. This multi-layered strategy manages intellectual property rights risk by expanding the border to fight counterfeiting, not only as cargo arrives at our ports of entry, but also internationally before cargo is laden on vessels destined for our shores, and after illicit goods arrive in our country.

- *Intellectual Property Rights Seizures Increase:* At mid-year FY 2010, intellectual property rights seizures are at almost 9,700, an increase of approximately 50% over mid-year FY 2009.

- *Supply Chain Management Program:* CBP hosted a kick-off meeting with private sector stakeholders on the development of a trade partnership to expedite entry of shipments into the U.S. that are at low risk for intellectual property rights infringement and to better focus CBP's inspection resources on shipments of high or unknown risk.

- *Intellectual Property Rights Targeting Models:* CBP coupled the expertise of its Intellectual Property Rights National Targeting and Analysis Group with new technology and targeting methods to build a new intellectual property rights risk model. In just completed testing, the model increased effectiveness in identifying shipments of counterfeit goods by a factor of four.

- *Applications for Intellectual Property Rights Enforcement:* CBP approved 862 applications, known as recordations, from trademark and copyright owners for CBP to protect their rights against counterfeit and pirated goods.

- *Technical Analyses:* Scientists in CBP's Office of Laboratories and Scientific Services have analyzed approximately 3,000 samples of suspected intellectual property rights-infringing products so far this year. These laboratory tests have resulted in seizures of products such as circuit boards, computer chips, video game systems, cigarettes, watches, perfumes and pharmaceuticals.

- *Foreign Training and Capacity-Building:* This year, CBP has traveled to Brunei, Cairo, Egypt, Bangkok, Thailand, Lima, Peru and Bamako, Mali to provide intellectual property enforcement expertise for regional training and capacity-building programs sponsored by the U.S. Government.

- *Enforcement Operations:* As a result of its targeting and interdiction successes, including targeting and interdiction for the IPR Center Operation Guardian and Operation Apothecary (see previous section), CBP continues to be the leading source of referrals to ICE for possible criminal investigations.

Immigration and Customs Enforcement

- *Operation Holiday Hoax:* Operation Holiday Hoax was a joint operation with CBP, the FDA and the USPIS that seized counterfeit goods in transit, at transportation hubs and at local retail sales points throughout the U.S. and Mexico. In the U.S., ICE and its partners seized more than 700,000 counterfeit items, with a total value of more than $26 million. Fifteen individuals were arrested in New York and Texas. Mexico's efforts resulted in the execution of 100 search warrants and the seizure of 274 tons of counterfeit goods.

- *Operation Spring Cleaning:* Initiated in April 2010, Spring Cleaning was an interagency intellectual property theft enforcement surge operation that targeted the manufacture, distribution and retail sale of counterfeit goods. Coupled with a simultaneous multi-national investigation in Baltimore, the two actions resulted in a combined total of 45 arrests and the seizure of 1.7 million items of counterfeit merchandise valued at $263 million.

- *Operation Global Hoax:* Initiated in May 2010, Operation Global Hoax is a multinational effort to identify, investigate and interdict the distribution of pirated movie and music products. Between

2010 JOINT STRATEGIC PLAN ON INTELLECTUAL PROPERTY ENFORCEMENT

May and July 2010, 35 countries around the globe will work with the WCO in this operation and exchange gathered intelligence in furtherance of this effort.

- *Operation Mercury II*: Operation Mercury II is a five-day surge operation planned for June 2010 to combat the importation and distribution of substandard and counterfeit pharmaceuticals. This operation will be a joint effort with the WCO.

- Between January and March 2010, ICE and CBP teamed with the NFL, NBA, NCAA, industry and local law enforcement to conduct operations targeting counterfeit sports merchandise sold during the Super Bowl, NBA All-Star Game, and the NCAA Final Four and Frozen Four tournaments. These operations resulted in seizures of over 14,000 items valued at more than $760,000.

- In April 2010, ICE announced partnerships with state and local law enforcement, resulting in the formation of 22 IPTETs, in which 70 federal, state and local law enforcement agencies have joined the 10 federal partners of the IPR Center in collaborating on activities to more effectively combat intellectual property theft nationwide.

- In early June 2010, ICE and the IPR Center, along with INTERPOL, co-hosted the 2010 Certification Industry Against Counterfeiting (CIAC) North America conference.

- In early June 2010, the IPR Center hosted a Symposium on International Organized Crime, Terrorism and Intellectual Property Theft, bringing together academia, industry, law enforcement and government.

- From January 1, 2010 through May 19, 2010, ICE's intellectual property theft enforcement activity resulted in 166 criminal arrests, 56 indictments, 34 convictions, and 1,078 seizures valued at more than $358 million.

Department of Justice

Over the past several months, DOJ spearheaded several key intellectual property initiatives:

- In February 2010, DOJ created a revitalized DOJ Task Force on Intellectual Property. The Task Force monitors and coordinates DOJ's overall intellectual property enforcement efforts.

- In March 2010, BJA posted its FY 2010 Intellectual Property Enforcement Program solicitation, making $4 million in funding available to state and local enforcement entities, including prosecutors, for intellectual property enforcement task forces and local intellectual property training and technical assistance. BJA anticipates, based on the $200,000 maximum award amount, awarding 20 field-initiated grants. The grants awarded in 2010 will build upon the previous intellectual property grant awards of nearly $2 million in August 2009 to eight state and local law enforcement agencies and two non-profit enforcement member organizations.

- On March 12, 2010, DOJ conducted an Antitrust Workshop: Agricultural and Antitrust Enforcement in our 21st Century—Issues for Farmers. The workshop included a panel that discussed how the patenting of genetically modified seeds has affected the competitive dynamics of the seed industry, and issues facing the industry as patents covering certain traits are nearing expiration.

- In April, 2010, DOJ announced the appointment of 20 additional FBI Special Agents dedicated to investigating intellectual property rights cases. These agents joined the 31 agents already deployed to field offices around the country devoted to investigating intellectual property crimes. As a result of these new appointments, the FBI created four enhanced intellectual property enforcement squads and increased personnel resources to six additional field offices.

- In April 2010, DOJ also announced the appointment of 15 new Assistant U.S. Attorneys positions devoted to prosecution of high tech crime, including computer crime and intellectual property offenses. The new positions will be located in California, the District of Columbia, Maryland, Massachusetts, Michigan, New Jersey, New York, Pennsylvania, Texas, Virginia and Washington.

- On May 26, DOJ participated in a first of its kind tri-agency workshop with the Federal Trade Commission (FTC) and USPTO (including high-level officials from each agency) on significant patent and antitrust issues that can have critical implications on innovation and competition. The workshop, labeled "The Intersection of Patent Policy and Competition Policy," discussed standard-setting, the patent backlog and the use of injunctions in district courts and at the ITC.

- During July, in coordination with USTR and FTC, DOJ will be holding an intellectual property/antitrust workshop for the Chinese antimonopoly agencies in China as part of our ongoing technical assistance.

- Over the past year, the Attorney General has also personally emphasized DOJ's renewed focus and efforts to combat intellectual property crime through cooperation with international law enforcement partners. On February 24, 2010, the Attorney General met with officials from the Rio De Janeiro Prosecutor's General's Office to emphasize the need for strong enforcement of criminal intellectual property laws and to develop stronger partnerships with Brazil as both countries seek to enhance their intellectual property enforcement efforts.

In addition to program-wide initiatives, DOJ has successfully participated in several high-profile intellectual property cases:

- In January 2010, a defendant was sentenced to 30 months in prison and ordered to pay $790,683 in restitution to Cisco Systems, Inc., as a result of his conviction for trafficking in counterfeit Cisco computer products. The defendant, a citizen of China, carried out the scheme while doing business as Gaoyi Tech, a company located in Shenzhen, China. The defendant procured counterfeit Cisco products in China in response to orders and then shipped the products to the U.S. [FBI]

- In 2009, an investigation uncovered a scheme to sell free-to-air satellite TV receiver boxes which would illegally decrypt Dish Network/Nagrastar signals and provide them free to the free-to-air receiver box purchasers. The main defendant hired computer hackers to break the encryption algorithm that Dish Network/Nagrastar used (know as Nagra 3) for placement into his free-to-air boxes. His co-conspirators received over $650,000 in payments from the main subject for their part in recruiting and trying to crack the encryption. Dish Network estimated its losses would have been more than $100 million if the subjects had succeeded in breaking the encryption. The three defendants pled guilty to conspiracy to violate the Digital Millennium Copyright Act. In January 2010, the main subject was sentenced to 18 months in custody followed by three years supervised release. The two co-defendants were sentenced to one month in custody and five months of house arrest. [FBI]

- In February 2010, DOJ filed a second brief in connection with the proposed class action settlement in the Google Books matter. (*The Authors Guild Inc. et al. v. Google* (S.D.N.Y.). DOJ submitted its views on the proposed settlement, indicating that the settlement raised class certification, copyright and antitrust concerns.

- In May 2010, two defendants were sentenced, respectively, to 10 years and one month in prison and seven years and 10 months in prison for roles in operating a major Internet-based DVD importation and distribution business as well as fraudulent receipt of government benefits. The defendants imported counterfeit DVDs in bulk from suppliers in the Philippines by means of false Customs declarations and sold them through websites. [FBI, USPIS and CBP]

- In May 2010, a man pleaded guilty to selling counterfeit cancer drugs using the Internet. The defendant admitted selling what he falsely claimed was the experimental cancer drug sodium dichloroacetate, also known as DCA, to at least 65 victims in the U.S., Canada, the United Kingdom, Belgium and the Netherlands. The defendant admitted that, in actuality, he sent victims a white powdery substance that was later determined through laboratory tests to contain starch, dextrin, dextrose or lactose, and contained no DCA. According to court documents, along with the counterfeit DCA, the packages also contained a fraudulent certificate of analysis from a fictitious laboratory and instructions on how to dilute and ingest the bogus DCA. DCA is an experimental cancer drug that has not yet been approved by the FDA for use in the U.S. [FBI]

- In May 2010, a defendant was sentenced to 51 months in prison and ordered to pay $119,400 in restitution to Cisco Systems, Inc. A Federal jury found the defendant, a Saudi citizen, guilty of charges related to his trafficking in counterfeit Cisco products. According to evidence presented at trial, the defendant purchased counterfeit Cisco Gigabit Interface Converters (GBICs) from an online vendor in China with the intention of selling them to DOD for use by U.S. Marine Corps personnel operating in Iraq. The computer network for which the GBICs were intended is used by the U.S. Marine Corps to transmit troop movements, relay intelligence and maintain security for a military base west of Fallujah, Iraq. [ICE]

- In May 2010, two defendants pleaded guilty to conspiracy to produce and sell counterfeit video gaming machines, commonly known as slot machines. The defendants admitted that they conspired to make and sell unauthorized copies of computer programs designed for video slot machines and counterfeit video slot machines bearing registered trademarks. One of the defendants was arrested in Riga, Latvia, and extradited from Latvia to the U.S. on Oct. 23, 2009. This defendant is the first individual to be extradited from Latvia to the U.S. under a new extradition treaty between the U.S. and Latvia, which entered into force on April 15, 2009. [FBI]

- In June 2010, two defendants were convicted after trial of importing more than 300,000 fake luxury handbags and wallets from China bearing counterfeit trademarks, including those of Burberry, Louis Vuitton, Gucci, Coach, Fendi, Chanel and others. The counterfeit luxury goods had an estimated worth of more than $100 million. At sentencing, the defendants each face a maximum of 30 years in prison and $4.75 million in fines. [ICE].

- In June 2010, DOJ's Antitrust Division filed a brief in a significant case involving patents, *In Re: Ciprofloxacin Hydrochloride Antitrust Litigation (Arkansas Carpenters Health and Welfare Fund v. Bayer A.G.)*, discussing the proper standard for evaluating "reverse payment" settlements of patent infringement litigation between branded and generic drug manufacturers.

Department of State

Counterfeit Medicines Initiatives: Undersecretary Hormats and EEB Assistant Secretary Francisco Fernandez launched a comprehensive initiative to combat counterfeit medicines. In consultation with industry and other agencies, DOS will focus part of its $4 million government-to-government training budget to build enforcement capacity in this specific area. A new public diplomacy initiative will fund outreach/public education activities in 25 countries.

Special 301 Contributions: EEB and Embassy Tel Aviv provided support for an extensive round of negotiations with Israel and Saudi Arabia, *e.g.,* reporting, information gathering, diplomatic contacts and logistics. The out-of-cycle reviews resulted in firm commitments for improved intellectual property regimes in both countries. DOS participated in the regular annual Special 301 review through reporting, analysis and strategy development.

Foreign Government Capacity Building: DOS-funded intellectual property rights law enforcement training and technical assistance (using Bureau of International Narcotics and Law Enforcement, Office of Crime Programs funds coordinated through a partnership with EEB-IPE) is currently being implemented by U.S. law enforcement agencies in countries around the world. Examples include the work of senior intellectual property advisors in Indonesia and the IPLEC in Eastern Europe, as well as regional training. Examples also include a March anti-counterfeiting workshop in Tanzania and a May intellectual property criminal enforcement training with INTERPOL in Senegal. A four-day workshop for Mexican officials in April reinforced recent legislative changes in that country. IPLEC training in Macedonia in February led to the largest raid in Macedonian history.

Public Diplomacy Initiatives: Undersecretary Hormats, EEB Assistant Secretary Fernandez, and many posts abroad participated in World Intellectual Property Day activities on April 26, highlighting the importance of intellectual property and DOS' commitment to protecting it. Many posts chose to screen the National Geographic "Illicit" video for local groups, including for the first time, a Spanish language version of the program.

Training State Employees: EEB, led by Assistant Secretary Fernandez, held an intensive training session for intellectual property officers in Western Hemisphere posts in January 2010. Industry and Washington-based intellectual property experts conducted a day of briefings and discussions of "lessons learned" in working intellectual property issues from an embassy perspective. Planning is underway for similar capacity-building sessions for intellectual property officers in Africa and Europe in the fall.

Executive Office of the President | United States Trade Representative

1/12/2010: USTR called for public comments on intellectual property protection and enforcement in preparation for release of the 2010 Special 301 Report.

1/26/2010: USTR led U.S. Delegation at the 7th round of the ACTA negotiations in Mexico.

2/17/2010: Following extensive USTR-led engagement, successfully concluded the Special 301 out-of-cycle review for Israel, leading to enhanced protection of data submitted to obtain marketing approval in Israel and improvements to Israel's patent regime.

2/24/2010: Following extensive USTR-led engagement, successfully concluded the Special 301 out-of-cycle review for Saudi Arabia, resulting in enhanced protection of pharmaceuticals and improved enforcement of copyrights.

3/3/2010: USTR held a public hearing on intellectual property protection and enforcement in preparation for release of the 2010 Special 301 Report.

4/6/2010: Following extensive USTR-led engagement, Mexico passed a law expanding ex officio authority for intellectual property enforcement (issue noted in 2009 Special 301 report).

4/12/2010: USTR led U.S. delegation at the 8th Round of the ACTA negotiations in New Zealand.

4/19/2010: USTR co-led U.S. delegation at U.S.-China JCCT intellectual property rights working group; urges stronger intellectual property enforcement.

4/21/2010: USTR released draft text of ACTA.

4/26/2010: Remarks by Ambassador Ron Kirk on World Intellectual Property Day.

4/26/2010: Remarks by Deputy U.S. Trade Representative Miriam Sapiro to the U.S. Chamber of Commerce Global Intellectual Property Center on World Intellectual Property Day.

4/30/2010: USTR released the 2010 Special 301 Report on intellectual property rights; announced removal of Czech Republic, Hungary and Poland from Special 301 Watch List due, in part, to stronger intellectual property enforcement achieved following extensive USTR-led engagement. The report included USTR's annual list of "notorious markets."

5/26/2010: Following extensive USTR-led engagement, the Philippines enacted a law to strengthen enforcement against illegal camcording in movie theaters (issue noted in 2010 Special 301 Report).

The Library of Congress | The Copyright Office

Consistent with its role of supporting the copyright enforcement activities of the U.S. Government, Copyright Office officials are frequent speakers at training programs and conferences, many of which include significant discussion of enforcement issues. Among the programs this year are the following:

- a speech about U.S. copyright developments for the Council of U.S. International Businesses in New York, NY on April 7;

- a speech on the topic of "Copyright and New Technology" on April 8 at the annual meeting of the American Bar Association in Crystal City, VA;

- a speech about current copyright developments for the annual intellectual property program hosted by the Special American Business Internship Program in Washington, D.C. on April 20;

- two presentations on current domestic and international policy issues of the Copyright Office on May 6 and 7 at the American Intellectual Property Association 2010 Spring Meeting in New York, NY; and

- a speech on ACTA and its negotiation as part of a panel of experts at the Future of Music Coalition's Policy Day in Washington, D.C. on May 25.

Performance Measures

Performance Measures: Data, Measures, and Indicators

It is important that the U.S. Government measure the effectiveness of this Joint Strategic Plan to protect and enforce the intellectual property rights of American innovators, creators, producers and workers. Such measurements convey to the public the impact of the U.S. Government's work and help the U.S. Government to continue and expand effective enforcement activities and fix or curtail ineffective ones. At the same time, it must be recognized that the goal—reduced infringement of intellectual property rights—is difficult to accurately measure, in large part, because infringers, like other types of thieves, try to hide their actions. This report sets out an initial list of key performance indicators for intellectual property enforcement, primarily measuring government activities. As the U.S. Government as a whole gains experience collecting and analyzing these indicators, further modifications or additional measures may follow. We intend to use these measures to track year-to-year changes to give some indication of whether the U.S. Government's intellectual property enforcement efforts are producing results.

Law Enforcement Actions

First, the IPEC, in coordination with the DHS, DOJ, HHS, and other relevant agencies will report on the number of enforcement actions involving intellectual property infringement.

Seizures

Second, the IPEC, in coordination with DHS, DOJ, and other relevant agencies will report on seizures involving intellectual property infringement.

Training/Outreach

Third, the IPEC, in coordination with DOC, DHS, DOJ, and DOS, and other relevant agencies will report on training and outreach by the U.S. Government involving intellectual property.

Increased Intellectual Property Protection in Other Countries

Fourth, the IPEC, in coordination with DOS, DOC, USTR, and other relevant agencies will report on changes in other countries in intellectual property protection.

Measuring Public Perceptions of Intellectual Property Rights

Fifth, the IPEC will work with DOC to explore the feasibility of using surveys to track public perceptions of intellectual property rights, particularly among key demographics (such as youth).

Appendix 1

History of the IPEC Office and Process Leading to this Joint Strategic Plan

On October 13, 2008, the PRO-IP Act created the position of the IPEC, placing it within the Executive Office of the President. As defined in the PRO-IP Act, the term "intellectual property enforcement" means "matters relating to the enforcement of laws protecting copyrights, patents, trademarks, other forms of intellectual property, and trade secrets, both in the United States and abroad, including in particular matters relating to combating counterfeit and infringing goods."

President Barack Obama nominated Victoria A. Espinel as the first IPEC on September 25, 2009, and the Senate confirmed Espinel on December 4, 2009. The Administration placed the IPEC within the Office of Management and Budget ("OMB"), in the Executive Office of the President. The office of the IPEC currently consists of the IPEC, one permanent employee, and four employees temporarily detailed from other federal agencies, including one each from: (1) DOC, USPTO, Office of the Solicitor; (2) DHS, Office of Policy; (3) DOJ, Civil Rights Division; and (4) DOJ, United States Attorney's Office for the Central District of California (Los Angeles), Cyber and Intellectual Property Crimes Section (CHIP Unit Attorney).

The PRO-IP Act directed the IPEC to submit to Congress a Joint Strategic Plan. To prepare this Joint Strategic Plan, the IPEC worked with: (1) OMB; (2) DOJ, including the FBI; (3) DOC, including ITA and USPTO; (4) USTR; (5) DOS; (6) DHS, including CBP and ICE; (7) HHS, including the FDA; (8) USDA; and (9) the United States Copyright Office. Additionally, the IPEC worked with other offices, including the Office of the Vice President, the Office of Science and Technology Policy, the Domestic Policy Council and the White House Counsel's Office.

The Joint Strategic Plan was formulated based on significant input from the public. In March 2010, the IPEC issued a FRN, seeking the public's input on: (1) the costs to the U.S. economy resulting from intellectual property infringement; (2) threats to public health and safety posed by intellectual property infringement; and (3) specific recommendations for fighting infringement, including ways the government could improve its effectiveness and coordination of intellectual property enforcement efforts. The Office of the IPEC received and reviewed more than 1,600 responses. To promote transparency, all of the responses were posted on the IPEC's website and are available for the public to review. *See* http://www.whitehouse.gov/omb/intellectualproperty/frn_comments/.

The IPEC also met with numerous companies affected by intellectual property infringement, organizations interested in intellectual property enforcement (both those seeking strong intellectual property enforcement and those seeking strong exceptions/defenses to intellectual property rights), trade associations representing industries for which intellectual property enforcement is important to their success, and labor organizations representing workers in affected industries. Most of these meetings took place in Washington, D.C., but the IPEC also traveled to cities and regions around the country to hear from industries affected by intellectual property infringement. The IPEC will continue to meet with the public to determine how well this Joint Strategic Plan is being implemented and to hear new concerns that arise.

Appendix 2

Literature Review

As part of the effort to craft the Joint Strategic Plan, the IPEC gathered data through several means, including through soliciting public comments in response to the FRN, collecting information on U.S. Government intellectual property enforcement-related spending through an interagency request and reviewing relevant literature.

The following is intended as a summary of submissions and studies and is not intended to be a U.S. Government endorsement of any specific study, methodology or data.

Summary of Data Received from Federal Register Notice Comments

The FRN issued by the IPEC in February 2010 requested that comments submitted identify costs to the U.S. economy resulting from infringement of intellectual property rights, both direct and indirect, including any impact on the creation or maintenance of jobs. The FRN provided guidance that data cited in the submissions should clearly state the methodology used in calculating estimated costs and any critical assumptions relied upon, identify the source of the data on which the cost estimates were based, and provide a copy of or citation to each such source.

Many of the comments submitted by organizations and companies representing specific industries reported economic data for those industry sectors. Such data included the number of jobs directly and indirectly generated by that sector, the average wages paid, sector-specific contribution to Gross Domestic Product (GDP), tax revenue and export data. For example, organizations from the semiconductor industry cite that the sector employs approximately 185,000 people in the U.S. and comprises the U.S.' second largest exporting industry.[1] According to the Business Software Alliance (BSA), the software industry in the U.S. employed 1.7 million people in direct and related industry positions, with wages that equaled 195% of the average U.S. income, and contributed more than $261 billion to the U.S. GDP in 2007.[2] Similarly, the Motion Picture Association of America reports that direct industry jobs had an average salary that was 26% higher than the national average and generated $15.7 billion in public revenues in 2008.[3]

Some submissions also identified the amount of investment made toward research and development (R&D). The Pharmaceutical Research and Manufacturers of America (PhRMA) reports that the biopharmaceutical industry invested $56.1 billion in R&D for new medicines, $44.9 billion of which was directed

---

[1] As reported by the Semiconductor Industry Association in its comments to the February 2010 FRN, and based on the ITC database (industry defined at a six digit North American Industry Classification System level.)

[2] As reported by the BSA in its comments to the February 2010 FRN, and based on the OECD STAN Database, available online at http://stats.oecd.org/Index.aspx?DatasetCode=STAN08BIS&lang=en. "Software and related services" are those businesses that fall under code 72 in the ISIC rev. 3 industry classification.

[3] As reported by the Motion Picture Association of America in its submission to the February 2010 FRN, and based on analysis of total jobs and wages (direct and indirect) using U.S. Bureau of Labor and Statistics (BLS) data and SIC to NAICS bridge, industry data, and the RIMS II model of the U.S. Bureau of Economic Analysis (BEA), and analysis of employment and payments data, using income and sales tax rates.

toward research conducted in the U.S.[4] In 2009, PhRMA estimates that industry investment in R&D was approximately $65.3 billion.[5]

A few organizations noted the need for balance in the U.S. Government's approach to intellectual property enforcement and for due consideration to be given to fair use of intellectual property rights. They cited the Computer and Communications Industry Association (CCIA) study from 2007 which reported that industries relying on the fair use doctrine generated revenue of $4.5 trillion and contributed $507 billion—18%—to U.S. GDP growth, generated $194 billion in exports, fueled productivity gains of $128,000 per employee and employed 17 million people.[6] The study provided total revenue generated by these industries, without defining which portion of the revenue resulted from use of intellectual property under the fair use doctrine.

Several submissions included numbers aimed at capturing the breadth of intellectual property in the U.S., highlighting, for example, that intellectual property-based industries account for more than $5 trillion of the U.S. GDP.[7]

Comments also offered estimates of the loss of jobs and revenue to the U.S. economy due to intellectual property theft. The most frequently cited studies were those from the Institute for Policy Innovation (IPI), which estimate that, annually, copyright piracy affecting the U.S. motion pictures, sound recordings, business software and entertainment software/video game industries cost the U.S. economy $58 billion in total output, 373,375 jobs, $16.3 billion in earnings, and $2.6 billion in Federal/state/local tax revenue.[8] Other submissions criticized these studies, contending that they relied on two unsubstantiated assumptions—that each pirated good represented a lost legitimate sale (a one-to-one substitution rate), and that jobs lost in one industry could not be replaced by jobs in other industries (no job migration)—that skewed the findings to overstate the impact of intellectual property theft on the U.S. economy.

Trends in Health, Safety, and Security

The FRN issued by the IPEC also requested that submissions identify threats to public health and safety posed by intellectual property infringement, in the U.S. and in other countries. The submissions identified a few intellectual property infringement trends related to health and safety issues, notably in the areas of pharmaceuticals; critical defense, and health and safety infrastructure; and activities in support of organized crime. The sections below provide a brief summary of those concerns.

[4.] The Biopharmaceutical Sector's Impact on the U.S. Economy: Analysis at the National, State, and Local Levels, Archstone Consulting, Lawton R. Burns, March 2009

[5.] Burrill & Company, analysis for PhRMA, 2005-2009, includes PhRMA research associates and nonmembers; Pharmaceutical Research and Manufacturers of America, PhRMA Annual Member Survey (Washington, DC: PhRMA, 1980-2009).

[6.] Computer & Communications Industry Association, *Fair Use in the U.S. Economy* (2007), http://www.ccianet.org/CCIA/files/ccLibraryFiles/Filename/000000000085/FairUseStudy-Sep12.pdf. Note that CCIA has recently published a 2010 updated version of the study.

[7.] Robert J. Shapiro and Kevin A. Hassett, "The Economic Value of Intellectual Property," USA for Innovation, 10/05.

[8.] Stephen E. Siwek, "The True Cost of Copyright Industry Piracy to the U.S. Economy", Policy Report 189, Institute for Policy Innovation, 10/3/2007.

Pharmaceuticals

Counterfeiting of pharmaceuticals can cause great harm and even death. Many counterfeits contain a dangerous amount of harmful chemicals which can cause serious adverse reactions. Others do not contain enough, or any, of the necessary active ingredients, thereby causing harm to patients who rely on these pharmaceuticals to overcome medical conditions and promoting drug-resistant diseases. On its face, it can be difficult to distinguish a counterfeit pharmaceutical from the legitimate product. Furthermore, the proliferation of pharmaceutical websites makes intellectual property enforcement in this area a significant challenge.

Organizations such as the Pharmaceutical Security Institute (PSI) collect and share information on counterfeit pharmaceuticals and help initiate enforcement actions. The Partnership for Safe Medicines (PSM) reported in its submission that, in 2009, PSI saw increased growth in the number of counterfeiting incidents globally, from 1,216 in 2006 to 1,585 in 2008, along with an expansion in the number of countries connected to such incidents.[9] According to the WHO, approximately "8% of the bulk drugs imported into the U.S. are counterfeit, unapproved, or substandard" and "10% of global pharmaceutical commerce, or $21 billion, involves counterfeit drugs."[10] LegitScript, an online pharmacy verification service, identified over 36,000 online pharmacies as of March 2010 that do not meet the standards for certification by this company.[11] PSM research indicates that the sale of all prescription pharmaceuticals online generated an estimated $15-20 billion in 2004.[12]

Critical, Defense and Health and Safety Infrastructure

Many submissions highlighted concerns that counterfeits are being found in products related to the nation's critical infrastructure, in defense technologies and in life-saving medical machines such as defibrillators and medical imaging equipment. The Semiconductor Industry Association (SIA) conducted a survey of its member companies in May 2007, and reported case-specific evidence of counterfeit semiconductors. One of the SIA member companies reported that a broker website indicated 40,000 of the company's devices being available; however the company had manufactured fewer than 200 units of that device. SIA notes several concerns with counterfeit semiconductors. Incorrect die or inserting the wrong chip into a system can lead to electronic system failure. Counterfeit chips being mislabeled as military-grade can lead to fatal malfunction in military and aerospace parts. SIA reports that while the military/aerospace market comprises less than one percent of the world market, this market is an attractive target for counterfeiters because it provides for particularly high profit margins due to the price differential between commercial and military-grade chips.

The submission by Underwriters Laboratories (UL), a not-for-profit product safety testing and certification organization, highlights a growth of counterfeiting in scope and product categories. UL states that increasingly sophisticated counterfeit products are being seized at U.S. ports at an increasing rate and

---

[9] As reported in the Partnership for Safe Medicines in response to the February 2010 FRN.

[10] Albert I. Wertheimer, et al, "Counterfeit Pharmaceuticals: Current Status and Future Projections," 43 J. Am. Pharm. Assoc. 710-8 (2003).

[11] As reported in the Alliance for Safe Online Pharmacies in response to the February 2010 FRN. *Also see* http://www.legitscript.com

[12] As reported in the Partnership for Safe Medicines comments in response to the February 2010 FRN.

reports that it has recently found unauthorized UL marks on healthcare appliances. WHO estimate that 6-8% of medical devices are counterfeit, or approximately $5.5-$7.3 billion in the U.S. market.[13]

Organized Crime

Several organizations including the Copyright Alliance have cited the 2009 report by the RAND Corporation's Safety and Justice Program and the Global Risk and Security Center. Through the study of 14 different cases, the report identified "a broad, geographically dispersed, and continuing connection between film piracy and organized crime" and links profits from motion picture piracy to 17 different organized crime rings in the U.S., Canada, Hong Kong, Italy, Japan, Malaysia, Mexico, Pakistan, Paraguay, Russia, Spain, Northern Ireland and the United Kingdom.[14] The report also documented film piracy as having been used to finance terrorist group activities in three of the 14 case studies, including those of Hezbollah, a group designated as a foreign terrorist organization by DOS.[15] The Alliance for Safe Online Pharmacies (ASOP) notes in its submissions examples of investigations, indictments or convictions linking counterfeiting of prescription drugs to terrorist organizations and organized crime networks.[16]

Summary of Additional Literature and Data

As part of the information and data collection effort, the IPEC also reviewed studies and reports, many of which were referenced frequently in the public submissions responding to the February 2010 FRN. Below is a summary of a few of these studies. The following is intended as a summary of submissions and studies and is not intended to be a U.S. Government endorsement of any specific study, methodology or data.

OECD Global Study[17]

The OECD global study on "The Economic Impact of Counterfeiting and Piracy" conducted in 2008, and subsequently updated in 2009, reported that trade in counterfeit and pirated products reached a value of approximately $200 billion U.S. dollars in 2005 (this number was later adjusted based on updated trade data to be closer to $250 billion). Some of the key findings and recommendations of the report are:

- That understanding the *primary market* and *secondary market* consumer trends and factors offers a framework within which to assess the propensity of a product to be counterfeit or pirated and can help guide quantitative research, and government and industry efforts.

- That the magnitude and scope of counterfeiting and piracy is larger than the national GDPs of 150 economies and affects nearly all product sectors.

---

[13] As reported in UL's comment in response to the IPEC FRN from February 2010.

[14] Gregory F. Treverton, Carl Matthis, Karla J. Cunnigham, Jeremiah Goulka, Greg Ridgeway, Anny Wong, "Film Piracy, Organized Crime, and Terrorism," The RAND Corporation Safety and Justice Program and the Global Risk and Security Center, 2009, http://www.rand.org/pubs/monographs/2009/RAND_MG742.pdf, pgs. xii and xiii

[15] Ibid., pg. xii

[16] ASOP provides links to two news stories (the links provided here have been updated from the FRN submission). *See* Ed White, "Detroit-area man guilty in cigarette scheme," *Associated Press* 1/12/2009, http://www.chroniclejournal.com/stories_oddities.php?id=157825; Reuters, "Counterfeit goods are linked to terror groups," International Herald Tribune, Feb. 12, 2007, http://www.nytimes.com/2007/02/12/business/worldbusiness/12iht-fake.4569452.html. Please reference ASOP's FRN submission for more references to such articles and reports.

[17] Information from "The Economic Impact of Counterfeiting and Piracy," OECD, 2008.

- That the effects are broad and profound and impact socio-economic environments, rightholders, consumers and governments. The study also reports that counterfeiting and piracy activities support criminal networks and organized crime.

Institute for Policy Innovation Studies

The IPI conducted three studies in 2006 and 2007 looking at the cost of piracy to the motion picture, sound recording and copyright industries in the United States. Notable statistics reported in the studies include:

- "The *total costs* to the U.S. economy of copyright piracy are estimated to exceed $58 billion in lost output, 373,375 lost jobs, $16 billion in lost employee earnings and more than $2.6 billion in lost tax revenues."[18]

- "Because of music piracy, the U.S. economy loses a total of $12.5 billion in economic output each year. Furthermore the U.S. economy also loses 71,060 jobs. […] As a consequence of piracy in sound recordings, U.S. federal, state, and local governments lose a minimum of $422 million in tax revenues annually."[19]

- "Motion picture and video piracy exact a heavy toll not only on the U.S. motion picture industry, but the overall U.S. economy as well: $20.5 billion annually in total lost output among all industries, $5.5 billion annually in lost earnings for all U.S. workers and 141,030 jobs that would otherwise have been created are lost. In addition, as a result of piracy, governments at the federal, state, and local levels are deprived of $837 million in tax revenues each year."[20]

These three studies used a U.S. Government-developed Regional Input-Output Modeling System ("RIMS II") to extrapolate and estimate direct and indirect losses to industry as a result of piracy.

NDP Consulting Study on Impact of Innovation and Intellectual Property on U.S. Economy

The NDP Consulting study on "The Impact of Innovation and the Role of Intellectual Property Rights on U.S. Productivity, Competitiveness, Jobs, Wages, and Exports" examines data of 27 U.S. exportable and importable industries during the 2000-2007 timeframe.[21] Of the 27 tradable industries assessed, 15 are intellectual property-intensive industries and 12 are non-intellectual property-intensive industries, based on measures of R&D expenditures, "as such expenditures are direct inputs for innovation and are the most widely used measures for intellectual property, enjoy higher productivity and greater competitiveness than non-intellectual property intensive industries."[22] The key findings of this study include:

- "IP-intensive industries create jobs and spur economic growth resulting from high investments in research and development (R&D) in comparison to non-IP-intensive industries. […] During

---

[18.] Stephen E. Siwek, "The True Cost of Copyright Industry Piracy to the U.S. Economy," Institute for Policy Innovation, 11/2007

[19.] Stephen E. Siwek, "The True Cost of Sound Recording Piracy to the U.S. Economy," Institute for Policy Innovation, 8/2007

[20.] Stephen E. Siwek, "The True Cost of Motion Picture Piracy to the U.S. Economy," Institute for Policy Innovation, 9/2006

[21.] Nam D. Pham, PhD., "The Impact of Innovation and the Role of Intellectual Property Rights on U.S. Productivity, Competitiveness, Jobs, Wages, and Exports," NDP Consulting, April 2010.

[22.] Ibid., pg. 52

2000-2007, IP-intensive industries spent almost *13 times* the R&D per employee that non-IP-intensive industries spent."[23]

* "IP-intensive industries sustain great long-term economic growth. […] Annual output (as measured by value-added) was $218,373 per employee in IP-intensive industries and only $115,239 in non-IP intensive industries."[24]

* "IP-intensive industries […] accounted for about *60 percent of* total U.S. exports."[25]

* "IP-intensive industries pay both highly-skilled and low-skilled employees more than non-IP-intensive industries. […] During 2000-2007, the annual salary of all workers in IP-intensive industries averaged about *60 percent higher* (1.6 times) than the workers at similar levels in non-IP-intensive industries."[26]

Economists Incorporated – "Engines of Growth Study"

Stephen E. Siwek authored a study in 2005 titled "Engines of Growth: Economic Contributions of the U.S. Intellectual Property Industries" which sought to quantify the economic contributions of certain intellectual property industries to the U.S. economy. In doing so, Siwek used industry-specific data that was organized based on the North American Industry Classification System (NAICS) and focused on three industry groups: (1) convergence industries—industries that participate in the creation and management of information in digital form (note that this grouping omits the motion picture and recorded music industries), (2) other patent industries—industries that rely on patent protection but are not considered convergence industries (such as chemical products, motor vehicles, and machinery), and (3) non-dedicated support industries—intended to capture certain industries' partial contribution to and support of the distribution of copyright and patent protected products.[27]

Key findings from this study were repeatedly referenced in the responses to the FRN, namely:

* "IP industries are among the largest and highest-paying employers in the country, representing 18 million workers who earn on average 40% more than all U.S. workers."[28]

* "For all IP industries, *gross exports* in 2004 exceeded $455 billion."[29] Given the DOC's ITA reported value of total U.S. exports in 2004, $814,874,653,655, one could calculate that intellectual property industries accounted for more than 50% of U.S. exports, a statistic that has been referenced by U.S. Government officials and industry.

Computer & Communications Industry Association—"Fair Use in the U.S. Economy"

The Computer & Communications Industry Association (CCIA) 2010 study on "Fair Use in the U.S. Economy" looks at the economic contributions of industries that benefit from fair use, the provisions of U.S. copyright law that allow for limitations and exceptions. Highlights from the study include:

---

23. Ibid., pg. 4
24. Ibid. pg. 5
25. Ibid., pg. 6
26. Ibid.
27. Stephen E. Siwek, "Engines of Growth: Economic Contributions of the U.S. Intellectual Property Industries," Economists Incorporated, 2005, pgs. 9-13
28. Ibid., pg. 1
29. Ibid., pg. 4

- "In 2007, fair use industries generated revenue of $4.7 trillion, a 36 percent increase over 2002 revenue of $3.4 trillion.

- Fair use related industry value added in 2007 was $2.2 trillion, 16.2 percent of total U.S. current dollar GDP.

- Employment in industries benefitting from fair use increased from 16.9 million in 2002 to 17.5 million in 2007. About one out of every eight workers in the United States is employed in an industry that benefits from the protection afforded by fair use.

- Exports of goods and services related to fair use industries increased by 41 percent from $179 billion in 2002 to $281 billion in 2007."[30]

Department of Commerce Assessment of Defense Industrial Base

In January 2010, DOC issued a study that provided statistics on "the extent of the infiltration of counterfeits into U.S. defense and industrial chains."[31] DOC gathered survey data from 387 companies and organizations across the procurement supply chain, covering the 2005-2008 timeframe. The data showed that "39% of companies and organizations participating in the survey encountered counterfeit electronics during the four-year period. Moreover, information collected highlighted an increasing number of counterfeit incidents being detected, rising from 3,868 incidents in 2005 to 9,356 incidents in 2008. These counterfeit incidents included multiple versions of Department of Defense qualified parts and components."[32]

GAO Report on Quantifying the Economic Effects of Counterfeit and Pirated Goods[33]

Title V of the PRO-IP Act required the GAO to conduct a study on the impact of counterfeit goods on the manufacturing industry and on the U.S. economy. The GAO confined its analysis to "the impacts of counterfeit and pirated goods on the economy and industries of the United States."

Based on its review of literature and meetings with experts (but no independent analysis), the GAO concluded that, while it may be extremely difficult to quantify the effect of counterfeiting and piracy on the economy as a whole, primarily because data on these illicit activities are hard to obtain, "counterfeiting and piracy is a sizeable problem, which affects consumer behavior and firms' incentives to innovate." It noted that this problem "is of particular concern as many U.S. industries are leaders in the creation of intellectual property."

Specifically, the GAO concluded that counterfeiting and piracy slowed growth of the U.S. economy, reduced innovation, and caused a decline in trade with countries having weak intellectual property enforcement. The report acknowledges that there are several "negative effects" on industries including lost sales, lost brand value and reduced incentives to innovate, but found that these effects vary widely among sectors and companies. It found that, as a result, the U.S. Government loses tax revenue, incurs

---

[30.] Thomas Rogers and Andrew Szamosszegi, "Fair Use in the U.S. Economy," Computer & Communications Industry Association, 2010, pgs. 8-9
[31.] U.S. Department of Commerce, "Defense Industrial Base Assessment: Counterfeit Electronics," 01/2010, pg. i
[32.] Ibid., pgs. i-ii
[33.] United States Government Accountability Office, "Intellectual Property: Observations on Efforts to Quantify the Economy Effects of Counterfeit and Pirated Goods," GAO-10-423, April 2010

intellectual property enforcement expenses, and that counterfeit goods pose risks to national security and to public health and safety.

On the other hand, the GAO questioned the piracy rates estimated by certain industry groups and certain assumptions and methodologies used in those studies. For example, the IPI studies employ RIMS II multipliers, which the GAO notes "assume(s) no job immigration or substitution effect."[34] In reviewing the OECD study, the GAO reports that the OECD itself stated that "one of the key problems is that data have not been systematically collected or evaluated and, in many cases, assessments 'rely excessively on fragmentary and anecdotal information; where data are lacking, unsubstantiated opinions are often treated as facts.' […] most of the international trade data were supplied by national governments and relevant industries, and the OECD did not independently assess the reliability of these figures."[35]

Budget Data Request FY2009-2011

The IPEC sent out a BDR to relevant U.S. Government agencies engaged in intellectual property enforcement to collect data on agency resources and other information pertinent to such activities. Data collected included a brief description of department or agency intellectual property enforcement programs; budget amounts allocated and obligated in FY 2009, estimated amounts for FY 2010, and planned amounts for FY 2011; personnel dedicated to intellectual property enforcement in FY 2009 (and estimated and planned numbers for FY 2010 and FY 2011);[36] performance metrics used by the department or agency to measure enforcement success; and any budget request for additional intellectual property enforcement funds for FY 2011. The IPEC will conduct annual BDRs, using consistent measures in order to allow for multi-year comparisons.

[34.] Ibid., pg. 23

[35.] Ibid., pgs. 16 and 24

[36.] The BDR asked departments and agencies to provide the total number of personnel available to work on intellectual property enforcement regardless of the number of hours actually spent on such enforcement. It also asked departments and agencies to provide the total number of Full-Time-Equivalents (FTEs) dedicated to intellectual property enforcement. To calculate the number of FTEs, departments and agencies were asked to compile the number of hours actually spent on intellectual property enforcement divided by the number of working hours in a year.

Appendix 3

List of Acronyms

ACTA	Anti-Counterfeiting Trade Agreement
APEC	Asia-Pacific Economic Cooperation Forum
ASEAN	Association of Southeast Asian Nations
AT&L	Acquisition, Technology and Logistics, U.S. Department of Defense
BDR	Budget Data Request
BJA	Bureau of Justice Assistance, U.S. Department of Justice
CACP	Coalition Against Counterfeiting and Piracy
CBP	Customs and Border Protection
CCIPS	Computer Crime and Intellectual Property Section, U.S. Department of Justice
CHIP	Computer Hacking and Intellectual Property, U.S. Department of Justice
CIAC	Certification Industry Against Counterfeiting
CLDP	Commercial Law Development Program
CPSC	Consumer Product Safety Commission
DCA	Sodium Dichloroacetate
DCIS	Defense Criminal Investigative Service
DEA	Drug Enforcement Administration
DHS	U.S. Department of Homeland Security
DOC	U.S. Department of Commerce
DOD	U.S. Department of Defense
DOJ	U.S. Department of Justice
DOS	U.S. Department of State
ECTF	Electronic Crimes Task Force
EEB	Bureau of Economic, Energy and Business Affairs, U.S. Department of State
ESA	Economic and Statistics Administration
EU	European Union
FAS	Foreign Agricultural Service, U.S. Department of Agriculture

FBI	Federal Bureau of Investigation
FCS	Foreign Commercial Service, U.S. Department of Commerce
FDA	Food and Drug Administration
FRN	Federal Register Notice
FTA	Free Trade Agreement
FTC	Federal Trade Commission
FY	Fiscal Year
GAO	Government Accountability Office
GBIC	Cisco Systems, Inc. Gigabit Interface Converters
GSA	General Services Administration
GSP	Generalized System of Preferences
G-20	Group of Twenty Finance Ministers and Central Bank Governors
HHS	U.S. Department of Health and Human Services
ICE	Immigration and Customs Enforcement
INTERPO	LInternational Criminal Police Organization
IOC-2	Organized Crime Intelligence and Operations Center
IPE	Office of International Intellectual Property Enforcement, U.S. Department of State
IPEC	Intellectual Property Enforcement Coordinator
IPLEC	Intellectual Property Law Enforcement Coordinator
IPR Center	National Intellectual Property Rights Coordination Center
IPRU	Intellectual Property Rights Unit, Federal Bureau of Investigation
IPTET	Intellectual Property Theft Enforcement Teams, Immigration and Customs Enforcement
ITA	International Trade Administration, U.S. Department of Commerce
ITC	International Trade Commission
NAAG	National Association of Attorneys General
NASA	National Aeronautics and Space Administration
NCIS	Naval Criminal Investigative Service
NIH	National Institutes of Health
NOI	Notices of Inquiry
NPRM	Notices of Proposed Rulemaking

NSC	National Security Council
NTIA	National Telecommunications and Information Administration, U.S. Department of Commerce
NW3C	National White Collar Crime Center
OCDETF	Organized Crime Drug Enforcement Task Forces
OCI	Office of Criminal Investigations, Food and Drug Administration
OECD	Organization for Economic Co-operation and Development
OIPR	Office of Intellectual Property Rights, U.S. Department of Commerce
PRO-IP Act	Prioritizing Resources & Organization for Intellectual Property Act (2008)
PWL	Priority Watch List
QHSR	Quadrennial Homeland Security Review
RISS	Regional Information Sharing Systems
SADC	Southern African Development Community
SBA	Small Business Administration
SME	Small and Medium Sized Enterprise
TPP	Trans-Pacific Partnership
TRIPS	Trade-Related Aspects of Intellectual Property Rights
USAID	U.S. Agency of International Development, U.S. Department of State
USDA	U.S. Department of Agriculture
USPIS	U.S. Postal Inspection Service
USPTO	U.S. Patent and Trademark Office
USSS	U.S. Secret Service
USTR	U.S. Trade Representative
VIPPS	Verified Internet Pharmacy Practice Sites
WCO	World Customs Organization
WHO	World Health Organization
WIPO	World Intellectual Property Organization
WTO	World Trade Organization

www.ingramcontent.com/pod-product-compliance
Lightning Source LLC
Chambersburg PA
CBHW081707310526

45790CB00021B/2429